A NEW ERA IN U.S. HEALTH CARE

A NEW ERA IN U.S. HEALTH CARE

Critical Next Steps Under the Affordable Care Act

STEPHEN M. DAVIDSON

stanford briefs
An Imprint of Stanford University Press
Stanford, California

Stanford University Press
Stanford, California

©2013 by the Board of Trustees of the
Leland Stanford Junior University.
All rights reserved.

Printed in the United States of America
on acid-free, archival-quality paper

Library of Congress Cataloging-in-Publication Data

Davidson, Stephen M., author.
  A new era in U.S. health care : critical next steps under the Affordable
Care Act / Stephen M. Davidson.
     pages cm
  Includes bibliographical references.
  ISBN 978-0-8047-8700-0 (pbk. : alk. paper)
  1. Health care reform—United States. 2. United States. Patient Protection
and Affordable Care Act. 3. Medical policy—United States. 4. Health
insurance—United States. I. Title.
  RA395.A3D384 2013
  362.10973—dc23   2013005362

  ISBN 978-0-8047-8723-9 (electronic)

Typeset by Classic Typography in 10/13 Adobe Garamond

FOR HARRIET,
WITH LOVE AND GRATITUDE
FOR SO MUCH OVER SO MANY GOOD YEARS

CONTENTS

PROLOGUE

In the spring of 2010, I published a book about the U.S. health care system. It described how the system works and the problems that result from its operation. I made the case that those problems needed to be solved because they threatened the system's future and were undermining the ability of Americans to get good care when they needed it—even when they had health insurance.

Moreover, I argued, the solution required that the federal government take a large role because the national system as a whole needed to change—and more quickly than if we relied on the normal evolutionary process built by the accumulation of individual actions. The main reason for both reform and a large federal role in it was that existing system dynamics were leading inevitably to further *system* deterioration even though each individual and each group were making decisions they thought were best for them.

The book also demonstrated that the origin of the problems lay primarily in dysfunctional incentives faced by all parties to the system—employers, insurers, individuals and families, providers of services, and even federal and state governments. All were making choices they thought were rational for themselves, at least in the short run, but when added together, those choices created problems for the system and the nation. Any real solutions, therefore, needed to include changes to those incentives, especially as they affected utilization decisions made by patients and their doctors.

Finally, I discussed the politics of reform, drawing key lessons from the history of the many prior attempts at system improvement. The central conclusion: no matter how compelling a case could be made on the merits, real reform faced an uphill legislative battle, making passage of a new law designed to produce comprehensive system change a long shot at best.

Yet in March 2010, against all odds, President Barack Obama was able to get the Congress to pass the Patient Protection and Affordable Care Act (ACA). Two weeks before the book appeared, he signed it into law.

The main purpose of this new book is to consider the future of the health care system—still struggling with the problems described in the previous book, but now with the advantage of the tools provided by the ACA. In Chapter One, I will summarize briefly the problems faced by the health care system so that we will be able to assess the likely impact of the ACA when it is fully implemented. Then, in Chapter Two I will describe the new law so that we can understand the new obligations and opportunities available under the Act. Chapter Three considers the question of whether, given its imperfections, passing the Affordable Care Act was a good idea. That consideration includes a discussion of the political opposition to the new law, which will affect the ability both to implement it and to improve it. And, finally, in Chapter Four I will examine several important issues that will help to determine the ACA's ultimate accomplishments: the role of Medicaid and the states; the implementation process; the creation of health insurance exchanges in the states; and the use of a new organizational form, accountable care organizations. I have selected these issues because they will have such a large role in determining the extent to which the ACA achieves its aspirations. If they and other provisions work as intended, doctors, patients, insurers, and others can over time actually change the health care system for the benefit of all Americans. It won't be quick, but we will be moving in the right direction.

Any book project that hopes to finish in a reasonable time requires help, and I have been fortunate to have had the assistance of two talented Boston University undergraduates. Both were admitted to the seven-year B.A./M.D. program and are now students at the Boston University Medical School. They are Ankit Agarwal and Ashwini Kerkar. They were enthusiastic, energetic, and creative in helping me locate useful references and were generous in offering their comments and questions as well, unintimidated by the differences in our age and experience. I am the beneficiary of their intelligence, insights, and hard work.

I have also been fortunate to work again with Margo Fleming, senior editor at Stanford University Press. She suggested the concept for this book and envisioned it as an early entry in the Press's new Stanford Briefs series of relatively short books for professionals and educated laypeople on important topics in a variety of fields. I was delighted to take her up on the idea, which I viewed as an opportunity to examine the health system challenges laid out in the earlier book, *Still Broken,* in the context of the Affordable Care Act. Margo was a pleasure to work with, not least because of her patience and support during my recuperation from the total hip replacement I needed after having broken my original one in a fall while playing tennis. I got to see firsthand the health system when it operates as all of us hope it will, with competence and efficiency, and produces a perfect result. Unfortunately, however, it set our schedule back by two-and-a-half months, during which Margo expressed encouragement but never impatience.

Finally, I am blessed to be able to acknowledge again the great debt I owe Harriet, my wife and partner for many years. We have not only collaborated professionally but together raised a wonderful family—now well into a new generation—travelled the world, and shared a life with more high points than can be enumerated. I am forever grateful for all she has done for and with me over our many years together.

A NEW ERA IN U.S. HEALTH CARE

1 HEALTH SYSTEM PROBLEMS

SUMMARIZED

Most everyone agrees that the many problems affecting health care in the United States can be grouped under three broad categories: access, cost, and quality. Some disagree, however, with the idea that the problems require a solution in which the public sector plays a large role or, alternatively, about what that role should be. To be able to assess for ourselves these and other difficult issues, we first need to come to an understanding about the problems in some detail.

Health system problems can be defined either by focusing on stories of individuals who, much as they would like to, are not able to use the health services they need or by reciting aggregate statistics that describe system problems at the national level. Some people are much more energized by one approach; some by the other. In the next few pages, I will summarize the problems using both approaches.

THE INDIVIDUAL PERSPECTIVE

There are three main reasons why Americans may lack access to needed services. One is that they live in areas with an inadequate supply of doctors, hospitals, and other professionals and facilities.

These tend to be people living in rural areas where the population is too sparse to allow health care professionals and facilities to sustain themselves financially. Although this is an important part of the overall problem, we will not concentrate on it here.

A second reason is that they do not have health insurance. Personal income for most Americans has stagnated over many years, failing even to keep pace with inflation. One result is that they tend to have limited income to pay for even routine medical services when these become necessary. Moreover, some medical services are expensive. For both reasons, therefore, most people need insurance to help them pay for needed services. By pooling relatively small monthly payments from many purchasers, an insurer accumulates the funds it will need to pay the bills of those subscribers who use services. Those monthly premiums are supposed to be manageable for the individuals who pay them, while the cost of treating a serious injury or illness tends to be more than all but a few can pay for with ready cash. Here are two additional points about insurance: one is that as the cost of care escalates, monthly insurance premiums rise, making coverage unaffordable for many and thus adding to the rolls of the uninsured. The other is that for the insurance pool to work, the insurer needs to enroll many who are healthy and will use few, if any, services. That is the way small monthly payments from lots of subscribers can grow into a fund that is large enough to enable the insurer to pay for expensive surgery or lengthy hospital stays. This is another reason, therefore, that it is critical to keep down the cost of health care itself: if the insurance becomes too expensive, then healthy people won't buy it—not because they cannot afford it, but because it seems like a bad deal: paying a lot of money for coverage even though they do not expect to use medical care in the first place. If the low users of services drop out, then the funds in the pool will have been contributed only by high-service users. In effect, each of the expected high users will be prepaying in installments the entire amount of funds needed to pay for their own care. Most are not able to do that, however, which is why others need to contribute to the pool too. If insurance works as intended, instead of prepaying, those who use services will get care worth more, maybe even a lot more, than they put in. That works because those who do not get sick will have paid into the pool as well but not taken anything out since they will not have used care. What everyone—users and nonusers alike—buys when he or she buys insurance is the peace of mind that comes from knowing that in the unlikely but possible event that they need expensive services (because they got hit by a drunk driver or developed cancer, for example), they will not need to worry about whether or not they can afford the services their doctor recommends.

Most Americans obtain their insurance through their employment. Typically, employers offer one or more health insurance plans, and employees sign up for coverage. Even employed people may lack insurance, however—for some the reason will be that their employers decide not to offer coverage. Overall, in 2010 69 percent of U.S. employers offered insurance to their employees.[1]

But among employers in 2010, 99 percent of those with two hundred or more employees did so, while only 59 percent of those with three to nine workers offered coverage. Many small employers simply decide the cost is too high for them to afford. Other workers lack insurance because, even though their employer offers it, they cannot afford their share of the premium. In still other cases, the worker may be covered, but not members of his or her family. Finally, of course, there are the unemployed and the almost 690,000 elderly who are not eligible for Medicare benefits. Despite all this, however, the fact is that 78 percent of uninsured Americans live in households with at least one member who works full-time (62 percent) or part-time (16 percent).[2]

Jonathan Cohn, in his book *Sick: The Untold Story of America's Health Care Crisis—and the People Who Pay the Price,*[3] tells numerous heart-wrenching stories of Americans who toil at several jobs in order to be able to afford health insurance. In many cases, despite working long hours for multiple employers, people find themselves priced out of the private market for health insurance and are unable to obtain it for themselves and their families. In some cases, as a fall-back position, they qualify for Medicaid, the federal-state safety-net program. But then they can lose that coverage when the state, in a budget-cutting move, changes the eligibility criteria or limits the covered services. At that point, having done everything right, they must throw themselves on the mercy of the local hospital and hope that staff there will provide the care they need. These tales are hard to read. The stories they tell tug at the heartstrings of readers with any sense of empathy, and they lead many to ask, "Isn't there a better way?" There must be something that the richest nation on earth can do to end this kind of unfair suffering!

Finally, a third reason why millions of Americans lack access to needed medical care is that although they do have insurance, they deny themselves needed services because the out-of-pocket costs (that is, the amounts not covered by the insurer—the "cost-sharing") are too high. To illustrate this point, here is a story that I recounted in my earlier book.

> Allen Orozco of Nashville, Tennessee, bought health insurance for his family—including his wife, Heather, and their three children—through his job with a mortgage company. The problem was that although his share of the premium cost him $800 each month—a struggle, but one they chose to endure—the coverage included a $1,500 per person deductible for each family member and then it paid only 80 percent of the cost of most diagnostic tests and surgical procedures. These provisions caused the Orozcos serious difficulties. Though young, Allen had asthma and an inflammatory bowel condition called Crohn's disease, and Heather had a serious gall bladder condition. Her doctor recommended that she have surgery to remove her gall bladder, and Allen needed expensive medications on an ongoing basis, with the possibility of surgery looming in his future, too. Even with insurance, the out-of-pocket cost of their care was more than they could handle, and neither one could afford to follow completely their doctors' recommendations.

Since Allen was the sole breadwinner while Heather was finishing school, they decided to do what they could to take care of his condition first. But the deductible for his prescription medications was so high that he "stretched them out" to make them last longer even though, by doing so, he undermined their effectiveness and recognized he was playing "Russian roulette" with his life. In the meantime, she got *no* treatment for her gall bladder condition. It frequently woke her up in the night with severe nausea, depriving her of the sleep she needed to carry out her responsibilities, which included getting the children ready for school and being a student herself. More than once, when her condition deteriorated to the point that she could no longer endure the pain, she wound up in a hospital emergency room—at a cost to the insurer of five or six times the cost of regular appropriate care in her doctor's office.

Unfortunately, the Orozcos' story is becoming all too typical.[4] These are people living the American dream—job, school, family—and it is all being threatened by inadequate health insurance. Health care spending has increased so much that the cost of insurance has led many firms to drop it for their employees. Others, like Allen Orozco's employer, cut it back in order to be able to offer at least some coverage. But those cutbacks resulted in deductibles and co-insurance payments that are so high that, as with the Orozcos, they keep families from getting the care the insurance is supposed to make accessible. Imagine what their story would be if—like at least 49.9 million other Americans—the Orozcos had no insurance at all!

Here is the bottom line: the inexorable increase in health care spending is putting both insurance coverage and health care itself beyond the grasp of more and more Americans. Moreover, these trends are now reaching deeper into the middle class.[5] Indeed, given the growth in spending, even organizations with historically comprehensive insurance plans, such as universities, are cutting back. In fact, many of those policies, though still in place, have been eroding for years. That erosion may take the form of rising premiums and cost sharing or the addition of prior authorization requirements that need to be satisfied before people can access many covered services.

THE AGGREGATE PERSPECTIVE

For many Americans, stories of individual suffering do not lead logically to proposals for corrective public policy. Some believe that people find themselves in these difficult circumstances, at least in part, because of their own failures; or that, whatever the cause, the solution is their own responsibility. They should find a job with better health insurance. Or maybe they would not have gotten sick in the first place if they didn't smoke or drink or eat too much. Years ago, this phenomenon was defined as "blaming the victim." Others *are* willing to entertain public policies to help people overcome these hardships, but are not sure that the stories being recounted define a problem that is large enough to require changing big chunks of the U.S. health care system, which they think of as the best in the world.

So instead of looking at stories of individuals who lack access to insurance or to care for one reason or another, the latter group wants to discuss the situation in the aggregate. When they make the effort to do so, among the facts they uncover are the following (summarized in Table 1.1):[6]

- The United States spends more money on the health sector than any other country—by a lot. In 2010, it was $2.6 trillion, which equaled 17.9 percent of GDP. No other country spent more than more than 12 percent of GDP.

- Those big numbers translate to about $8,402 per capita— twice as much as the next most expensive country. If there are four people in your family, that adds up to $33,608. When you realize that these averages include families with almost zero spending on health care, it becomes clear that, for some families, the cost of services used can be truly huge, well beyond the financial reach of most of us. In fact, this possibility should make it clear why having health insurance is a good idea for any family's peace of mind and financial well-being.

- The rate of spending *growth* has been substantial for years. When Medicare and Medicaid became law in 1965, health care spending equaled only about 5 percent of GDP, not even close to 2010's 17.9 percent.

- Out-of-pocket costs—those not covered by insurance—are the highest in the world, too, also by a lot. They were 29.1 percent of spending in 2009.

- Furthermore, even though we spend a lot, *many Americans have no insurance coverage at all*. As of 2011, 18 percent of the non-elderly population was uninsured. The number tends to grow when economic times are hard. That is a big reason why Medicaid rolls, as well as the rolls of other counter-cyclical safety net programs, grow during those times.

- Millions are *under*insured. They do have coverage, but it is too skimpy for them to get the care they need. Like the Orozcos. The only policies they can buy require out-of-pocket payments when they use services that cost more than they can afford. The percentage of non-elderly adults who are underinsured exploded from 12.3 percent in 2003 to 22 percent in 2010, just seven years later.

- Many people want insurance, but are rejected by insurers because they had prior conditions that insurers thought would cause them to be high users of services in the future. Wendell Potter puts that number at more than 650,000.[7] Insurers either refused to cover them outright or charged so much that people could not afford coverage.

- And for many years, students of the health care system have had great concern about the *quality of medical care*. Donald Berwick, the former head of the Center for Medicare and

Medicaid Services (CMS), the federal agency responsible for these two big programs as well as for much of the Affordable Care Act, has devoted his career to finding ways first to assess the quality of care and then, building on that knowledge, to improve it.

- The clearest evidence that we still have serious quality problems, although many claim that much progress has been made in recent years, is that national studies show great variation from state to state in aggregate measures of quality.[8]

Whether you consider the problems of individuals or the aggregate condition of the U.S. system as a whole, the conclusion is inescapable that the U.S. health care system has serious problems. Using the common shorthand, they fall into the three main categories mentioned earlier: access, cost, and quality.

The critical point is that the problems are with the system as a whole, and the federal government is the only institution that can deal with the entire system. Therefore, if you agree that the problems need to be solved, it seems to me inescapable to conclude that the federal government must play a substantial role in improving the situation. Incremental changes adopted by one group or another—employers, insurers, physicians and other providers—even if they were fundamental enough and on a grand enough scale to cause the needed improvements throughout the

TABLE I.I.
Selected data on health care spending, 2010

National Health Expenditures, 2010		
In billions of dollars	$2,593.6	
As percentage of GDP	17.9%	
Per capita	$8,402	
Out-of-Pocket Spending	29.1%	2009
Uninsured (non-elderly)	18%	2011
Underinsured (non-elderly)	22%	

system, would drag out the reform process for too many years. In the meantime, the scale and scope of the problems would continue to escalate. Others disagree, and indeed, the argument about the proper role of government in reforming the health care system has been going on for many years. In fact, partly for that reason, until Barack Obama did it in March 2010, no president except Lyndon Johnson in 1965, following a huge electoral victory the year before, has been able to persuade Congress to adopt a comprehensive reform plan.

Usually we describe the problems in the ways I just did—either that individuals are suffering from lack of coverage or that the system denies access to too many, spends too much, and produces care of a quality that is too unreliable. But we also need to understand something about how the system actually works.

THE PROVIDER PERSPECTIVE:
HOW THE SYSTEM WORKS

Up to this point, we have considered primarily either the system's impact on individual citizens who at various times and for many reasons need health care services, or alternatively, the measures that reflect national spending on health care or aggregate measures of quality and other concerns about the actual services provided. Instead, we could examine the situation as faced by health care providers—organizational ones such as hospitals and medical group practices and individual clinical professionals practicing in small neighborhood doctors' offices. When we do that, we can learn a lot about how the system operates now and how I believe it is likely to continue to function over the next five to ten years. A key fact is that all of them tend to operate *under great financial pressure*.

First of all, *insurers do not cover provider costs*. It may be obvious, but it costs doctors' practices money to provide care to their patients. They rent space, buy or lease equipment and supplies, and hire staff. To make a go of it financially, those providers must charge fees that not only cover these costs but include amounts to replace outdated equipment, get help when their computers don't work properly, attend courses to update their knowledge and skills, and, of course, earn a living that supports their families. Costs for larger health care organizations can be even more. Yet insurers do not pay provider charges. Private insurers have tended to pay higher rates than public-sector payers and Medicare more than Medicaid, but no one pays provider charges, which presumably are set to at least cover their costs. Until recently, I was on the board of a small, not-for-profit health center on Block Island in Rhode Island, and the patients who paid amounts closest to the center's charges were those who paid directly out of their own pockets—that is, those without insurance. They paid about 90 percent of charges. The state's Blue Cross/Blue Shield plan paid about 75 percent. United Healthcare, another private insurer, and Medicare paid about 65 percent. This is an untenable situation— for everyone. Providers, especially small primary care practices like that one, struggle to make ends meet.

Provider costs may be higher than they should be because many providers are considered to be pretty inefficient in day-to-day operations. That may be true, but the fact is that most provider organizations do not really know what the relationship is between their costs and their charges. This observation has long been made not only about small community-based medical practices, but also about many hospitals.[9]

Even without inefficiency, however, costs for individual services provided tend to increase every year. The reason is that the inputs into those services tend to increase—testing supplies, prescription drugs, and professionals' time, among other things, go up in cost every year.

Another contributor for some providers is that some patients have no insurance and cannot pay much, if anything, for the services they use. Some put off seeking medical care until they can afford it. But not everyone can do that. And providers, especially hospitals, must treat them—at least until a clinician can determine that the patient's condition has stabilized.[10]

So, given this set of difficult circumstances, how do health care provider organizations cope?

One of the most common ways is to increase the volume of services they provide—but not just to anyone. Providers tend to want patients with good insurance and with diseases or conditions on which they can make money. The fact is that some services are profitable, and others are not.

Some providers may also try to cut their costs and increase their efficiency. But there are problems with that approach, too. For example, many believe that investment in information technology (IT) can improve both the quality and efficiency of care. Actually, although this is the conventional wisdom, and the federal government has made millions of dollars available as grants to spread the use of IT throughout the medical care system—it offers other incentives, too, in the form of higher payments for practices that use IT—the jury is still out on IT's actual effects.[11] Research is inconclusive in part because it is difficult methodologically to plan studies that can demonstrate unequivocally that IT is the cause of whatever improvements are found. Regardless, however, the adoption of IT is expensive. And to the extent that there actually is a payoff—in improved efficiency, for example—the benefit tends to go to the payers, not the providers. That is, if a provider organization reduces duplication of services, an important source of unnecessary spending, as a result of an electronic medical record (EMR), it will earn less because it will be providing fewer services and therefore insurers will be paying them less. Thus, even though they will have invested about $40,000 per physician for the EMR and another $10,000 annually for the ongoing technical support they will need, *the practice will earn less income*.[12]

Utilization of services is the process that generates spending. Therefore, utilization patterns must change if spending is to be contained. That means doctors will need to make different recommendations to their patients about the services their patients should use than they have been making to date. In that context, another obstacle to positive change is that managers have had little influence over physicians' clinical decision making unless the physicians were employees of the organization, which is not usually the case. Not only do physicians tend to know more about the clinical issues than managers, but because they usually earn a fee for each service they provide, they *benefit* from *in*efficiency. So does the medical practice or other care-giving organization that the managers run. Indeed, the hospital, too, may benefit from inefficiency because it, too, earns money for services provided, even for unnecessary ones.

It is worth taking a few minutes on clinical decision making because utilization decisions are the key to both cost containment and quality improvement. (We will draw on this discussion in Chapter Four as well when we consider accountable care organizations.) Although in the current system many patients do not visit doctors when they should for reasons already discussed—with the new law, that should change—once patients actually do see a doctor, they tend to do what the doctor recommends unless they cannot afford to do so (like Allen Orozco). So what factors do doctors consider in making clinical decisions?

When a patient visits a doctor, he or she expects the physician's primary, if not sole, interest to be to provide information, advice, and other services on the basis of an expert professional assessment of the patient's clinical condition.[13] Moreover, patients expect to pay (either directly or with insurance) for that information and advice and those related services, thus providing their doctors with the income they need to sustain their practice and to support themselves and their families. That income may come as separate fees for services rendered, as salary, or as part of a monthly capitation fee for each insured patient paid to the health care organization or plan for which the physician works as a partner or an employee.

It is now well established not only that all of those methods of paying physicians have distinctive incentives but also that patterns of physicians' clinical decisions reflect those incentives to some degree.[14]

The problem has two parts. First, in many if not most instances, there is not one, single clinical solution that is supported by incontrovertible evidence and about which all knowledgeable physicians would agree. Moreover, the extent to which any given physician can draw on his or her own direct knowledge of the patient's presenting clinical problem—whether from the literature or personal clinical experience—varies considerably. For example, primary care physicians see patients with many different complaints. They may recognize and know how to treat successfully the ones they see most commonly, but at the same time, may have trouble with symptoms they see only rarely. As a result, conscientious physicians may disagree as to what information and recommendations are likely to be most beneficial to a particular patient. This is true, in part, because of the physicians' limited experience with the set of symptoms and because of variations in their access to information that can help them fill in the gaps in their knowledge.

The situation is complicated further by the second part of the problem: the fact that payment methods give physicians a second interest in addition to their interest in meeting the medical needs of their patients. The reason is simple: physicians can benefit personally from (or be harmed by) those financial arrangements regardless of whether or not their actions fully meet the needs of their patients. Moreover, at least some physicians recognize this potential conflict. In a recent survey, 21 percent of American physicians *disagreed* with the following statement: "Doctors should put patients' welfare above the doctor's own financial interests."[15]

Thus, in this context of clinical uncertainty, when physicians provide information and make clinical recommendations for a patient, it is reasonable to ask, "Whose interest takes precedence—the patient's or their own?" Or "Under what conditions does the physician's primary interest shift from that of the patient to his own?" These straightforward questions reflect the possibility that a common, perfectly understandable financial transaction in which patients pay physicians for services rendered (either directly or through insurance) may actually deflect physicians from meeting their patients' expectations that the information they provide and clinical recommendations they make are in the patients' best interest.

These are not new questions. Rather, they reflect issues and controversies of long standing. If medicine is "in essence a moral enterprise . . . built on ethically sound foundations,"[16] how can one explain the "profound unease with the seeming primacy of economic factors among those currently affecting medical practice in the United States" especially since "[t]here is general agreement that patients' interests must take precedence over physicians' financial self-interest"?[17] Moreover, while the physician's financial interest is the non-clinical factor that gets the most attention, it is not the only factor that has the potential to influence his or her clinical decisions. Some of the others can increase the probability that the physician's recommendations will be in the patient's best interest, while still others might tend to divert the physician from that goal. Given the clinical uncertainty and the presence of competing influences on physician choices, "genuine medical professionalism is in peril."[18]

In fact, questions relating to both the extent and appropriate role of professionalism have been attracting increasing amounts of attention in recent years. Indeed, the question arises as to whether professionalism can even be an effective force any more in helping to resolve contemporary conflicts.

In the next few paragraphs, I will articulate an ideal type of physician-patient interaction—that is, what I believe most people would like to experience when they visit a physician. Then I will identify a group of potential influences on physician decisions that may interfere with the attainment of that ideal.

THE IDEAL ARRANGEMENT

Mark Pauly, an economist at the University of Pennsylvania's Wharton School, has argued that patients visit doctors for their expertise.[19] They have a pain or discomfort, but since they often cannot name it and do not know what (if anything) to do about it, they go to a doctor to obtain answers to their concerns that are based on the physician's expert knowledge. What that patient expects is that the doctor will ask whatever questions are relevant and conduct whatever tests are appropriate, and that, in providing information, making his or her recommendations, or providing services directly, he or she will be thinking only of what is best for the patient. Although patients may not realize how unsettled the scientific basis is for much of the "information" or recommendations they are provided, the last thing a patient wants is for doctors to consider the effect on their own income as they make decisions regarding what services have the best chance to improve that patient's health. Moreover, since every service carries a degree of risk (even if a small one), rational patients do not want doctors to administer tests that do not help make an accurate diagnosis or to provide services that do not treat the condition effectively. But, by the same token, they do not want their doctors to withhold tests or services that would benefit their health.

Instead, patients want their doctors to provide information and base their recommendations on expertise gained from their formal education, supervised clinical training, updated evidence from the research literature, and accumulated practice experience about what tests are important and what treatments work.

In practice, however, doctors, like other people, are influenced by a wide range of factors. In addition to their medical knowledge and the financial incentives associated with a payment method, doctors may also be influenced by the impulse that led them to choose medicine as a career in the first place, typically a desire to help people. And they may be influenced by the professional standards learned during their training and reflected in codes of ethics adopted by the medical societies to which they belong. Or they may be influenced by licensing laws and related regulations intended to guarantee that the public is well protected, some of which may incorporate those professional codes of ethics. In the United States at least, they may also be influenced to some degree by the threat of malpractice claims.

Further, as I noted earlier, some doctors work in organizations as partners or employees. Those organizations receive payments from patients or insurers and then, out of that income, must pay the personnel and other expenses associated with the provision of services. Thus they have a finite income with which to meet their legal and ethical obligations to serve patients. Partly for that reason, therefore, they hire managers whose job includes arranging for needed staff, appropriate facilities, and necessary supplies for the organization's clinicians to carry out their responsibilities. In addition, part of their job may also include ensuring that the doctors and other clinicians who are responsible for the clinical "product" offered by the organization perform according to standards that are consistent with the organization's ability to succeed both clinically and financially. Therefore, managers who are concerned about the quality of care provided as well as the cost of delivering it may try to influence decision-making processes in the hopes of improving the quality and efficiency of services delivered.

In sum, these factors may intervene—in ways and to an extent that are unclear—between the physicians' medical knowledge and the clinical decisions they make (see Figure 1.1).[20]

All of this is background. In this chapter, I discussed the U.S. health care system's problems and made a case for public policies that can improve access to services and quality of care as well as contain costs. And I also identified the main target of change—utilization patterns—and the clinical decisions, made primarily by

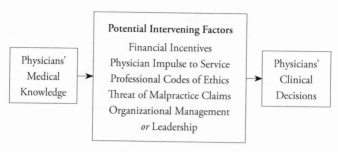

FIGURE I.I.
Preliminary list of influences on patient-physician interactions

doctors, that will produce those better utilization patterns. In the next chapter, I will describe the Patient Protection and Affordable Care Act that the president signed in March 2010 and some of the ways it might address the challenges we face in trying to produce beneficial changes to the U.S. health care system.

2 THE PATIENT PROTECTION AND AFFORDABLE CARE ACT OF 2010

The Affordable Care Act (PL 111-148) became law on March 23, 2010. Reflecting both the complexity of the health care system and the law's multiple goals, it is over nine hundred pages long and includes many different provisions scheduled to become effective at various points beginning six months after the president signed it.[1]

The overarching purpose of the Affordable Care Act (ACA) is to stimulate and facilitate important changes in the U.S. health care system in order to (1) make its services accessible to all Americans, (2) increase the chances that people will actually benefit from buying insurance and using services, and (3) keep spending under some degree of control. The centerpiece of the overall strategy to accomplish those goals is reform of the private insurance sector.

THE PRE-ACA PRIVATE SECTOR SITUATION

Before describing provisions related to private health insurance, it is important to note that over the past twenty-five years or so, the private health insurance sector has transformed itself from a field dominated by the *not-for-profit* Blue Cross/Blue Shield plans that operated in states throughout the country into a largely *investor-owned* industry. The investor-owned companies, many of which grew dramatically by buying Blue Cross plans and converting them to for-profit firms, had acted very aggressively in their local or regional markets. Several of the most successful ones then ventured into other regions to purchase and convert still other Blue Cross plans. The result is that in 2006, just under 50 percent of non-federal insurance coverage was held by investor-owned companies.[2] That percentage has undoubtedly grown since then.

Because, as for-profit companies, these health insurance firms are committed to earning ever-larger profits in order to grow their share price and to reward investors, it is especially important to understand how they make their money. Their *revenues* are the payments made by employers and individuals to purchase health care coverage as well as money earned from investing those premiums before the cash is needed to pay for medical services. Their *costs* consist of (1) the money they spend to operate the firms and (2) the cash they pay out to providers of the services used by their subscribers. Their *profits*, therefore, are the share of revenues left over after they pay for the company's operation and especially for the services used by the people they insure. Their principal challenge comes from the fact that the amount to be spent on medical care is much less predictable than that spent on administration, which includes promotion and sales, compensation for employees (including high executive salaries and bonuses), and information technology.

That point is true even though the insurers have actuaries who are able to calculate the probable number of broken bones, heart attacks, and cancers among a large group of insured people with known characteristics (such as age, gender, smoking history, prior use of services, and other factors). And they can also calculate the number of physician visits, blood tests, colonoscopies, open-heart surgeries, hospitalizations, and prescriptions to be expected in the coming year given what is known about the customers who have bought their insurance policies.

The actuaries calculate probabilities for a group of subscribers on the basis of what they know about subscriber characteristics and prior health history. So an employer with a young, healthy workforce may be charged $X per member per month, while a firm with an older workforce of the same size may be charged $X + $100 per member per month. The reason is that, simply on the basis of age, older workers can be expected to use more services, and therefore their employers will cost the insurer more than the employer with a younger workforce. With more information about the covered lives—for example, the presence of prior medical conditions—actuaries can make even more precise estimates. Yet, while the information they have is good for setting premiums, especially for large customer groups, insurers could be adversely affected if one of the predicted cancer patients happens to turn up among a small firm's young, healthy workforce instead of in the larger firm's older group of workers. The fact is that the actuaries do *not* know exactly which individuals in the group will exhibit any particular symptoms or use any specific services in the coming year. Nor, indeed, can they say with certainty whether any patients at all will actually be diagnosed with cancer. Their predictions are especially problematic in small firms. They have a much better chance of being correct if the insured group is large. Regardless, however, all the actuaries can do is predict the probabilities for the group as a whole, on the assumption that this year's experience will be a lot like last year's experience.

If the employer's firm is small, that single cancer patient could be the difference between a profit and a loss for that risk group. Or the company with the younger workforce might be hit by unexpectedly high expenses because two employees and their wives were on their way to dinner one evening when the car they were riding in was rammed in the side by a drunk driver speeding through a red light and all four passengers suffered major injuries. The point is that in a small group, a few cases that are both unexpected and expensive can throw off the most sophisticated calculations and dramatically reduce the insurer's profit for a particular employer or customer. And that is especially the case when the number of covered employees is relatively small.

As a result, insurers do whatever they can to increase the predictability of the amount spent on medical care, which, as noted, is the least predictable component of its expenses. Among the more benign tactics they have used, one is to favor large employers over smaller ones when seeking customers. The reason is that, as just noted, this year's experience of a company with several thousand employees is much more likely to be like last year's than that of a firm with only a hundred employees. In addition, the unexpected but expensive event will have a smaller impact on the finances of the larger company's insurer than the smaller company's carrier. These considerations are important to an insurer's strategy development because typically an insurer must cover *any* employee of the customer firm who wants to buy coverage from it (that is, it may not exclude particular individuals in the employer group).

Insurers are more concerned about the individual and small-group markets in which the experience is inherently much less predictable than the market for large employers. The tactics they have used to reduce the unpredictability of their experience in those markets include refusing to sell to individuals with prior conditions, refusing to pay bills for care received (and provided in good faith by clinical professionals who usually check a person's coverage before treating him), and cancelling coverage for people who get sick (called "rescission").

PROVISIONS OF THE ACA

The ACA contains reforms designed to combat the insurer tactics described in the previous section, as well as others. Thus it includes the following: insurers are prohibited from imposing annual or lifetime limits on the dollar value of benefits; from cancelling coverage once in effect—unless the covered individual intentionally misrepresented a material fact about his or her condition (that is, committed fraud); and from excluding people because of preexisting conditions or other health status characteristics. In addition, renewability of coverage must be guaranteed; all health insurance offered must include the comprehensive set of health benefits that are described in the law and will be specified further by the Secretary of Health and Human Services (HHS); and the waiting period before coverage becomes effective may not exceed ninety days.

Even in the individual and small-group markets, insurers must offer plans that cover the "essential health benefits" identified in the law and which will be defined further by the Secretary of HHS in regulations. Deductible amounts must be limited to $2,000 per year for self-only coverage and $4,000 per year for other coverage. And insurers must offer plans with only four levels of coverage, which are defined by the percentage of the actuarial value of the benefits provided. The four levels are bronze (60 percent of the actuarial value of benefits), silver (70 percent), gold (80 percent), and platinum (90 percent). Further, total cost sharing—which includes deductibles, co-insurance, and copayments—is limited to the dollar amounts for self-only and family coverage that are in effect under the Internal Revenue Code of 1986. These amounts change periodically.

Premiums in the individual and small-group markets may vary only as a result of the following conditions: whether the plan covers an individual or family; the rating area (that is, geography); age (but not more than three to one for adults; and tobacco use. In other words, insurers may not charge high prices to individuals with preexisting conditions in order to discourage them from buying coverage. The only exception is age. Finally, insurers in the individual or small-group markets must spend 80 percent of their premium income on medical care or quality improvement efforts, and those in the large-group market, 85 percent. Prior to the law's being passed, many for-profit insurers spent less than those amounts on medical care and more than 20 percent or 15 percent, respectively, on administration, salaries, and profits.

These and other provisions in the law make it much more likely that people who buy insurance, especially in the individual and small-group markets, will be protected from the kinds of practices that private insurers have used in recent years to grow their profits, and thus that they will actually benefit from their purchase of health insurance.

In 2009, during the development of the ACA that passed the Congress in March 2010, representatives of the health insurance industry agreed to the reform conceptualization which is now embodied in the law. Their agreement was critical in getting the legislative process off the ground—although as negotiations progressed, they became less enchanted with some provisions and withdrew their support.

Since what I have described so far are provisions that reduce insurers' ability to limit their risk and thus secure their profits, a natural question is, Why would they agree to these types of changes? The answer lies in other provisions of the law. And to understand them, we need to know more about the U.S. health care system.

Reducing the Number of Uninsured

One of the most salient characteristics of the U.S. health care system, as noted in Chapter One, has been the fact that substantial numbers of Americans have been uninsured. The United States is the only industrialized country in the world that does not guarantee health insurance coverage to its people. Not only is that harmful to the uninsured themselves who, as a result, have less access to the health care they need, but as I demonstrated in my earlier book, it causes many other dysfunctional effects of the U.S. health care system.

Therefore, one of the goals of the ACA is to reduce dramatically the numbers of Americans who are uninsured. The mechanism for accomplishing that goal is a requirement that virtually all Americans buy health insurance coverage. This is the so-called "individual mandate." Its presence creates a number of challenges, which need to be solved elsewhere in the law and which will be discussed further on. But its main effect is to create a very large expansion of the private health insurance market. Insurers considered that to be enough of a potential benefit that it neutralized their unhappiness over the provisions just discussed.

The mandate is important for at least two reasons. First, insurers need a large and diverse risk pool because, as noted, the essence of insurance is that well people subsidize the sick people who use services. Sharing the risk is the underlying principle of insurance. Thus the risk pool needs to include lots of people who use few services in order to have enough money to pay for the care of the few people who need either lots of services or expensive services. Without those healthy people, premiums would need to be much higher and, as a result, fewer employers would offer coverage and fewer individuals would buy it. If that happened, the numbers of uninsured Americans would grow, not shrink. So the mandate is needed to maximize the size and diversity of the risk pool.

But second, Americans with limited disposable income might be tempted to skip buying health insurance in order to save their money for goods or services that they consider more important, at least in the short run. After all, health insurance is needed primarily when people get sick. Many young, healthy people doubt they will get sick enough to need care that they will not be able to afford without insurance. When they make that assumption, they are overlooking the possibility of being hit by a drunk driver or suffering a broken bone in a basketball game. If healthy people do not buy insurance, then the people who do buy it will disproportionately be those who have risk factors—such as preexisting conditions—that make them more likely to need services. If that happens, the premiums will need to be higher in order to grow a fund that is large enough to cover the services used. And higher premiums will make it even less likely that healthy people with limited incomes—and who don't expect to use it—will buy it. This phenomenon is known as biased (or adverse) selection.

Therefore, in order to have the largest, most diverse risk pool and the lowest possible premiums, a mandate is needed.

But there are two other problems that must be solved for the reform to work. One is that too many people with limited incomes may truly not be able to pay the full price for their insurance even if per capita prices are kept down by a large, diverse risk pool. So their ability to buy coverage must be subsidized.

In addition, the market needs to be organized in such a way as to reduce the probability—if not avoid it altogether—that insurers will take advantage of unsophisticated purchasers who don't know what coverage they need and have trouble determining whether the policy offered by company A is better than the one offered by company B. For that reason, the law requires that the states create health insurance markets, called health insurance exchanges. Each state will create rules for companies that want to compete for customers in that state. (Groups of states may form regional exchanges). In those states that fail to create their own exchanges, the federal government may step in and create them so that all Americans will be covered no matter what state they live in.

The exchanges will ensure that all the firms that offer policies cover the comprehensive set of benefits specified in the law and by the Secretary of HHS, charge reasonable prices, and describe their offerings in simple terms using presentation formats that maximize the ability of consumers to compare them. Firms that fail to live up to the rules would need to adapt or would be forbidden to offer plans in the exchange.

A question that might be asked is, What happens if insurance companies determine they cannot make enough money to satisfy their investors and decide to pull out of the market? That is, suppose some insurers are not willing to offer policies that conform to the provisions of the ACA. In theory, that would be okay. For one thing, that is the way markets are supposed to work. The opportunity to make a profit attracts companies to compete by offering products and services that they hope will be better or less expensive or both than those offered by other companies. When that happens, customers are satisfied and so are the company's investors and managers. When firms decide they cannot compete successfully—maybe they are not well enough organized or managed or maybe their coverage is too expensive—they can pull out of the market. In the extreme, if *all* firms dropped out, the field would be left to the federal government, which could step in and offer well-priced, comprehensive coverage like that available to the elderly and disabled through Medicare. Indeed, one option could be to expand Medicare to include residents of a state that has no competing private insurers. The federal government already knows how to operate that kind of a program and should be able to expand enough to add a state or two to its portfolio of offerings without too much trouble. Since the Medicare program is well run and administratively inexpensive, there is every reason to believe the state's residents would be well served if that happened.

Medicaid Expansion

Here then is the situation. Everyone is required to buy insurance. Most non-elderly Americans will get it, as now, through their employers. In addition, states will set up exchanges so that private insurers can compete for the business of those without access to affordable employer-offered policies. The policies they offer will need to cover the same specified comprehensive set of services and include only four actuarial offerings that, among other things, limit cost sharing and charge manageable prices. And subsidies would be available for those needing help to purchase coverage. The idea is that everyone will be able to act on the mandate, and the result will be coverage of upward of 90 percent of the population, a vast improvement over the situation today.

Even with subsidies, however, some people will not be able to afford private insurance coverage. For them—that is, people under age sixty-five whose family income does not exceed 133 percent of the poverty line for similar-sized families and who are not covered by Medicare—the ACA expands the federal-state Medicaid program. This is the program created in 1965 as Title XIX of the Social Security Act, the companion to Medicare, which is Title XVIII of the same Act. Medicaid's primary purpose was to provide financial access to needed medical care for low-income people. In the original law, they were defined as people who either were eligible for cash assistance under federal-state welfare programs or became eligible by "spending down" enough of their income on medical care to qualify. Medicaid required the states, which operated the program and shared the cost, to cover a comprehensive set of benefits, with some flexibility to determine their "amount, duration, and scope." Under the ACA, each state must provide "benchmark" or "benchmark-equivalent" coverage, which is defined as the standard Blue Cross/Blue Shield preferred-provider benefits available under the Federal Employees Health Benefits Program (FEHBP), coverage offered to state employees in that state, or coverage offered by the state's largest health maintenance organization. The intent is to provide coverage for a comprehensive set of services.

The cost of the Medicaid program is shared by the federal and state governments, with the "federal medical assistance percentage" (FMAP) ranging from 50 percent to 83 percent. A state's actual FMAP varies inversely with its per capita income. Thus poorer states get more help from the federal government than richer states. In that way, low-income people who happen to live in poor states would not be disadvantaged compared to their fellow citizens who are similar except that they happen to live in richer states.

From January 1, 2014, when the coverage expansion provisions are scheduled to take effect, the ACA provides that the federal government will pay 100 percent of the cost of covering those who are newly eligible for Medicaid as a result of the Medicaid-expansion provision of the ACA. After December 31, 2016, the federal government's share for covering those newly eligible Medicaid beneficiaries will decline, but will still be much higher than the previous FMAP for that state.

While expanding access to services is one of the law's important goals, ACA provisions also address the two other legs of the three-legged stool of access, spending, and quality. The latter two go together in that some of the provisions intended to improve quality can also have the effect of reducing spending. Moreover, the access provisions already discussed make it even more important that the cost versus spending and quality issues be solved, as well. Here is why: as noted, the ACA requires virtually all Americans to buy coverage and prohibits insurers from rejecting any applicant who wants to buy coverage from them. It also constrains both what insurers can charge—in part because of the competitive nature of the markets (that is, health insurance exchanges) to be created in all of the states. As a result, it increases the pressure on insurers, public as well as private, to contain the cost of the medical care. Not only are their revenues limited, but they must spend 80 percent or 85 percent of those revenues on medical care.

That is a tall order, and neither public sector programs nor private insurers have had consistent success in limiting their outlays on medical care. How can the insurers keep their spending down without undermining the quality of care being provided by clinical organizations and professionals?

First, we need to remember that the key is for clinicians, especially doctors, to make decisions (or recommendations to their patients) that effectively address the clinical problems that the patients they see bring to their visits. Knowing that, it is also important to recall that, for many conditions, there is no single correct treatment on which all knowledgeable clinicians agree and that many clinicians have limited experience with some of their patients' symptoms and illnesses. The combination of those last two points means that doctors need help in determining which tests to order, which drugs to prescribe, when a referral to a specialist is a good idea, and when hospitalization is the most appropriate choice.

PATIENT-CENTERED OUTCOMES RESEARCH

To help physicians and patients make good clinical decisions, the ACA created a private, nonprofit corporation called the Patient-Centered Outcomes Research Institute (PCORI) (see ACA section 6301 forward). The purpose of the Institute is "to assist patients, clinicians, purchasers, and policy-makers in making informed health decisions by advancing the quality and relevance of evidence concerning the manner in which diseases, disorders, and other health conditions can effectively and appropriately be prevented, diagnosed, treated, monitored, and managed through research and evidence synthesis that considers variations in patient subpopulations, and the dissemination of research findings with respect to the relative health outcomes, clinical effectiveness, and appropriateness of the medical treatments and services."[3]

PCORI is governed by a board that includes the director of the Agency for Healthcare Research and Quality, the director of the National Institutes of Health, and seventeen others representing patients, clinicians, private payers, pharmaceutical and device manufacturers, quality improvement or independent health services researchers, and federal and state governments. The Institute was created to fund research "that will provide patients, their caregivers and clinicians with the evidence-based information needed to make better-informed health care decisions."[4] It helps "people and their caregivers . . . make informed health care decisions" by supporting methodologically rigorous research to answer patient-centered questions such as the following:

"1. 'Given my personal characteristics, conditions and preferences, what should I expect will happen to me?'

2. 'What are my options and what are the potential benefits and harms of those options?'

3. 'What can I do to improve the outcomes that are most important to me?'

4. 'How can clinicians and the care delivery systems they work in help me make the best decisions about my health and health care?'"[5]

To answer these questions, the Institute supports research that

"• Assesses the benefits and harms of preventive, diagnostic, therapeutic, palliative, or health delivery system interventions to inform decision making, highlighting comparisons and outcomes that matter to people; [and]

• Incorporates a wide variety of settings and diversity of participants to address individual differences and barriers to implementation and dissemination."[6]

The work of the Institute is funded by the Patient-Centered Outcomes Research Trust Fund (PCORTF), populated with transfers from the general fund of the U.S. Treasury and fees imposed on Medicare, private health insurers, and self-insured plans.

The objectives are laudable but difficult to achieve because they depend on research methods that are evolving. In comparing alternative treatments for a particular clinical condition, for example, it is important to be sure that the patients are similar in all the ways that might affect outcomes, the samples are large enough to detect small differences, and the studies cover a long enough time that the outcomes have a chance to develop. For these reasons, it is likely that the benefits of patient-centered outcomes research will be limited at first and will grow over time as more studies are done and research methods improve.

COST CONTAINMENT EFFORTS

Many are concerned that while the ACA does much to improve access to needed health care, especially for the millions who do not have health insurance, it does not do enough to contain expenditures. Henry Aaron, the distinguished health economist at the Brookings Institution, disagrees, noting that "Congress created a broad and potentially powerful portfolio of cost-control instruments, containing virtually every method that analysts have advanced for slowing growth of spending in a rational fashion— accountable care organizations, comparative effectiveness analysis, bundled payments, value-based insurance design, limits on the exclusion of employer-financed premiums from personal income tax, and health insurance exchanges to promote competition among insurance plans."[7]

Much of the attention regarding cost containment has focused on another new organization called the Independent Payment Advisory Board (IPAB). It is to be a federal agency, whose fifteen members would be appointed by the president with the advice and consent of the Senate. The majority and minority leaders of the two houses of Congress would nominate three members each (that is, twelve of the fifteen members). All members would serve six-year terms, except that some of the initial appointees would serve for shorter periods in order to establish a stagger such that whenever terms expired, continuity would be provided by the majority of members who would continue on the board.

Under Section 3403 of the ACA, which creates the IPAB, the chief actuary of the Medicare and Medicaid programs is charged with calculating the annual per capita growth rate in Medicare expenditures as well as setting a target per capita growth rate for the coming years. If the actual annual rate is higher than the target rate for that year, the chief actuary would establish a savings target to bring it down. And the IPAB is charged with developing a proposal to accomplish that reduction. In doing so, the board is prohibited from rationing care, raising premiums, increasing cost sharing, or otherwise restricting benefits or modifying eligibility. Moreover, the Secretary of HHS is charged with implementing the IPAB savings proposal unless the Congress explicitly both rejects it and installs in its place other plans that would produce comparable savings. The provision is written in this way in part because of the history associated with the Medicare Payment Advisory Commission (MedPAC), which, over the years, has made many cost-saving proposals. But since it was created as a body to advise Congress and lacks any regulatory authority, MedPAC had to submit its proposals to the Congress, which has refused to enact them.

Even some progressives oppose IPAB, arguing that clinical decisions should be left in the hands of doctors and patients and not ceded to unelected public officials. Surely, it would be good if doctors made their clinical recommendations thinking only of their patients' best interests. The problem is that, as noted in Chapter One, other factors sometimes intrude and divert physicians from acting in that way. One of those factors is that, while sometimes they may choose the exact right service, doctors often select ones that are unproven or considerably more expensive than other services that do an even better job. In many cases, they make these choices because either researchers have not produced unambiguous results or doctors simply do not know the relevant evidence.

IPAB's job is to propose plans that would help Medicare meet its financial targets. If it finds services for which the evidence clearly shows that they would not achieve the clinical goals—and may be expensive to boot—it might recommend that those services not be eligible for Medicare payment in such situations. Their recommendations would indeed become effective and payment could be denied, *but only* if Congress failed to intervene with another strategy for accomplishing the same financial objectives. So while it is easy to raise the specter of "Big Government" intruding between a patient and his doctor, the reality is likely to be much more benign. And then add this consideration: members of IPAB, who will be quite aware of the controversy surrounding its work, are likely to exercise extreme caution in their recommendations in order to avoid undermining the board's legitimacy. If they act rationally, they are likely to err on the side of restraint and recommend nonpayment only when the evidence is unequivocal that a particular service is useless or much more expensive but no more effective than another service.

Finally, it should be noted that, at this writing, since the first members have not been appointed yet, and it has not begun work, it is too early to tell what IPAB's effects will actually be. Moreover, Republicans introduced legislation in the House to repeal the IPAB provision. And although it passed on March 22, 2012, it did not pass the Senate; and in the unlikely event it had, President Obama would surely have vetoed it. Senate Republicans have also said they would filibuster IPAB nominations, thus depriving the board of members. Finally, if it survives all these challenges, we will have to see whether it can develop proposals that will actually contain spending given the reality constraints it will face. Thus the IPAB story is far from over.

3 WAS THE AFFORDABLE CARE ACT A GOOD IDEA?

Should We Scrap It and Try for Something Better?

Comparing the outline of health system problems in Chapter One with the summary of the ACA's provisions in Chapter Two, it is apparent that the two are not a perfect match. The obvious questions are, Was passing the law a good idea? Should it be overturned in favor of a better plan? Since the law is not perfect, these are reasonable questions to ask. The answers are, to a considerable extent, matters of judgment, but those judgments can be informed by what we know.

In a few pages, I will discuss what we know and why, on the basis of that knowledge, I conclude that it is important to try to make the Affordable Care Act work. Before doing that, however, we must discuss another issue that could have made that consideration moot. I refer, of course, to the fact that twenty-six states filed suit against the federal government, challenging the ACA's constitutionality. Several cases made their way through the federal district courts and circuit courts of appeal to the Supreme Court. In November 2011, the high court agreed to hear them. It scheduled oral arguments for late March 2012 and ruled on June 28, 2012.

CONSTITUTIONAL CHALLENGES TO THE LAW

It was a foregone conclusion that the president's Republican opponents would oppose the law—not only during the legislative process, but even after they lost that round and the bill became law. I refer to the "president's Republican opponents" advisedly because the party's leadership made it clear it would oppose the president on virtually everything he tried. Congressional Republicans, in the words of their Senate leader, Mitch McConnell, said their main goal was not to find the best solutions to the nation's problems, but to deny President Obama a second term. To further that objective, their opposition to any of his proposals—even ones that previously had been championed by Republicans—was meant to deny him any possible policy successes that would undermine their overriding determination to make him a one-term president.

In the case of the ACA, the law's imperfections and the strategy for reform imbedded in it made attacking the law's constitutionality a logical post-passage tactic for them to pursue. The contribution of Republican governors to the strategy was to file the suits that challenged the law in the courts. Since some of the lower-court decisions affirmed the law's constitutionality while others denied it, the Supreme Court had to settle the matter.

I am neither a lawyer nor an academic student of constitutional law, so although I have read the commentaries of many experts, as well as some of the briefs submitted to the Supreme Court and the ruling itself, the views I am about to express are those of a layman.

First, no one challenged the claim made by the government that health insurance and health care are conducted in interstate commerce. Article One, Section Eight of the Constitution says that "The Congress shall have Power . . . To regulate Commerce with foreign Nations, and among the several States, and with the Indian Tribes. . . . " The final provision found at the conclusion of that section gives Congress the power "To make all Laws which shall be necessary and proper for carrying into Execution the foregoing Powers, and all other Powers vested by this Constitution in the Government of the United States, or in any Department or Officer thereof."

So, given that health care is interstate commerce and that Congress has the power to regulate interstate commerce as well as to make "all laws" that are "necessary and proper" for executing that power, why wasn't that the end of it? If the Congress decided that regulating health insurance and health care, which it clearly has the power to do, required adoption of the provisions at issue, why did that Congressional decision not establish the law as constitutional?

I suppose someone might say that Congress could have achieved its goals using another approach to reform and that, therefore, the specific provisions of this law were not "necessary." On the other hand, choosing to rely heavily on reform of the private insurance sector was certainly a reasonable approach to addressing health system problems. Moreover, a strong case can be made that it was even the *necessary* approach to follow, given the long, dismal history of trying to enact reform—that it was the most rational one because it had the best chance of actually passing. A plan that uses the private insurance sector undoubtedly had a better chance of making it through the Congress than one that, for example, would have expanded Medicare, a public-sector program, to include not just the elderly and disabled but everyone.

Then, having chosen that approach, the collective judgment of Congress was that the specific provisions adopted were, by definition, necessary. Among those provisions, the case for the individual mandate was that it gave private insurers their best chance to provide the intended coverage profitably enough to be willing to participate. Again, why was that not the end of it?

Let's look at the individual mandate itself. This provision requires almost all Americans to buy insurance either through their employer or through a health insurance exchange created by the states for people who do not have access to affordable employer-based coverage. Opponents argued that people cannot be forced to buy something they do not want even if a worthy public purpose would be served by doing so. As one of the justices suggested during oral argument, individuals can make rational decisions to refrain from buying health insurance—for example, if they are young and healthy, have a low probability of needing expensive services (even though everyone's probability is greater than zero), and would rather spend their money on other things.[1] He went on to say such people cannot be forced to enter a market in order that the market can be regulated.

The way I see it, all Americans are in the market for medical care—preventive services, acute care, or management of a chronic condition. They may not be *actively* seeking care at the moment, but when they get sick, their level of activity shifts from dormant to active. Similarly, when they want a mammogram or a flu shot or some other element of preventive care, they become active in the market for health services.

That being the case, rational people will also be thinking about how they will pay for those services when the need arises. They will naturally, therefore, consider buying health insurance, the lowest-cost way to pay for care, especially for expensive services. At that point, given the (presumably, low) probability of the need for care and the cost of the premium, young people with competing needs for their limited income might decide to take a chance and forego health insurance. Does that mean they did not enter the market? In my view, contrary to Justice Alito's suggestion, they did enter the market, but decided to put off until later the question of how to pay for care they might need.

Consider a purchase decision which may be more common and thus easier to relate to than the purchase of health insurance. Many of us with computers get to the point when we decide we want a new computer. The old one still works, but it is painfully slow and, since it is four or five years old, we worry that it may soon fail altogether, thus causing great consternation and possibly hardship. So we go to the store (or look online) for a new one that will be faster and more reliable, and with enough memory to accommodate newer versions of favorite programs. The constraint: we have only $1,000 to spend. After shopping around, we discover that the least expensive version with the features we want costs $1,400. What to do? The two main possibilities are to reduce our desires and be satisfied with a lesser model or wait until later when we have added $400 to our available funds.

If we choose option two, are we in the market? Certainly, searching for a machine counts as being in the market. What happens if we decide to wait until our financial condition changes? Have we left the market, planning to return, or are we still in it, but at a level of activity that has become dormant? I believe we are still in it because we are figuratively or literally setting aside funds to buy the new machine. How is this different from the hypothetical person who decides to put off considering whether conditions have changed enough to buy health insurance? In both cases the decision can be delayed, and in both cases the cost-versus-availability of funds is a critical consideration.

The market for health insurance was not created so that it can be regulated, as Justice Kennedy suggested. It already exists, and the person in the hypothetical case outlined by Justice Alito has decided simply to put off the purchase until later when he has more money or a greater need for care. Undoubtedly, if it turns out he needs care before he has a chance to buy coverage, he may have lost the chance to buy insurance and instead may be forced to come up with the cash. If he breaks his hip in a fall during his weekly basketball game, his bill for a replacement may be $20,000 or more.

In my view, therefore, he is in the market for health insurance, but put off a decision to buy it. A secondary point is that, if the need for service arises before he decides he can afford the insurance, he may not only have lost the opportunity altogether, but also be stuck with huge out-of-pocket medical bills. For him, in retrospect, the decision to not buy coverage earlier would seem to have been irrational—every year many people with a low probability of needing services turn out to need them while many with higher probabilities turn out to not need them. One might even be tempted to say that since everyone faces a non-zero probability of needing medical care and since the cost of those services can be quite expensive, the rational decision is always to find a way to buy insurance. Indeed, recognizing the reasonableness of the last point, the ACA contains provisions for subsidies and regulations that both reduce the cost of coverage and make particular insurance policies affordable for those with limited incomes.

It is also worth pointing out that those who decide not to buy insurance but then develop the need for services and are not rich enough to pay the full cost of care out of pocket are in effect choosing to let others pay at least part of the cost of the services they use.

Since a state government can force people who want to own a car to buy automobile insurance, why can't the federal government require those who will want to use health care (arguably, everyone) to buy health insurance? We do not need automobile insurance most of the time—just as we don't need health insurance most of the time. But when we get into an automobile accident, we want that auto coverage, and it is too late to buy it. Therefore, states require us to buy it in order to register the car. In the same way, it is too late to buy health insurance when a person needs health care services—despite the justice's suggestion that a rational consumer might do just that. Yet if it were possible to buy insurance closer to the time of needing care, the cost of that coverage would be too high for even more patients to afford. If the cost of the needed services is also too expensive, the effect will be that the patient is either not able to use the services he needs or, if he does get the care—say, in a hospital emergency room—the provider who furnishes it may not get paid. And if he does get paid, it will be because someone else—usually taxpayers—came up with the money. Surely that is not in any such individual's interest, whether patient or provider, and it is not in the public interest.

Opponents of the law don't see it that way. Their conceptualization, as the justice suggested, is that the person who decides not to buy insurance is making a rational decision to stay out of the market for insurance. By implication, the market for health services is separate and not at issue. In fact, however, as I have suggested, the markets for insurance and care are inextricably linked.

Moreover, since the need for medical care is unpredictable, even for people who are young and healthy—think about being hit by a drunk driver or being injured while playing a sport— many who make that "rational" decision will wind up needing services. And some of those services for some of those people will be more expensive than they can afford. By not buying insurance, they create problems for themselves, for the providers being asked to furnish the needed care, and for the society which will be stuck with the bill.

The public interest in everyone having insurance derives from several points. One is that if everyone has coverage, then the risk pool is as large, as inclusive, and as diverse as it can be. As a result, the price of coverage (that is, the premiums) can be as low as possible, which means that more people will be able to afford it without subsidy. That is the case because, as we saw earlier, the idea behind insurance is that everyone will pay a manageable amount on a regular basis (say, monthly) in order to build a fund that can pay for care. Then, as a result, no one will need to worry about the cost of needed services in the event that he or she gets really sick or has an accident and requires expensive care. What people are really buying when they buy health insurance is the peace of mind that comes from knowing that whatever services they turn out to need will be paid for. As the patient lies in a hospital bed following an accident in which he was hit by a drunk driver, he will not be forced to decide whether or not he can afford the life-saving services or surgery the doctor recommends. Indeed, that being the case, is it really "rational" for anyone to forego insurance?

Another benefit that comes from everyone having insurance is that providers of services—that is, the delivery system—will have stable financing. In the pre-ACA world, providers could expect to receive payment for patients who have insurance. But since so many people do not have coverage, they knew that treating some patients meant they either did not get paid at all or were paid only part of their expected fees. Moreover, the payments might have been stretched out over an extended period in order for the patient to have managed the cost of care.

Still a third benefit accrues to the insurers. If everyone has coverage, then the insurers will have gained millions of new customers. Even if the restrictions on coverage in the law constrain their ability to *maximize* the profit on individual accounts, as insurers argue, the large number of newly insured Americans should add substantially to their aggregate profits. The mandate, coupled with the creation of health insurance exchanges at the state or regional level, means that insurers will also benefit from the requirement that they use a common format to describe their offerings for potential customers. Doing so will simplify that aspect of marketing and reduce their administrative costs even though it may also force them to be more similar to their competitors than they might have been if those kinds of rules did not apply.

While it is not clear that the Supreme Court considered these reality factors in reaching its decision, the fact is that the Court's majority agreed that the individual mandate is, indeed, constitutional. However, a 5-4 majority determined that its legitimacy derived not from Congress's power to regulate interstate commerce, as suggested above, but from its power to tax, which gave it the ability to impose a penalty on those who failed to buy health insurance. In commenting about the decision, Jeffrey Toobin wrote that this "argument is not a persuasive one." Instead, he said, for seventy-five years "the Supreme Court has recognized that the Commerce Clause of Article I of the Constitution gives Congress a free hand to address national economic problems. And few national economic problems are bigger than those of the health-care system." Moreover, during that long period Congress "passed many laws that attempt to address health-care issues. Without exception, and without even much controversy, the courts have found those laws to be constitutional." As a result, he said, "this should have been an easy case."[2]

The Court's reasoning may have implications that we cannot yet know for future decisions on other constitutional issues, but, for our purposes, the important point is that the individual mandate stands, and reform of the private insurance sector can proceed as anticipated by the ACA.

Before leaving the Supreme Court's decision, we need to focus on another, rather unexpected, part of it. A 7-2 majority of the Court also held that the federal government cannot withhold the federal share of a state's Medicaid funds if a state's policymakers decide not to expand its Medicaid program to accommodate all state residents with incomes below 133 percent of the federal poverty line.

For many years, when the federal government wanted states to accept or share responsibility for achieving a public purpose, it offered the states money to help pay for it. That is, the federal government offered a "grant in aid" to those states that met the law's conditions. Implicitly, a state might decide not to accept the federal government's offer. And, indeed, using Medicaid as an example, when Title XIX of the Social Security Act became law in 1965, states were offered federal money to cover part of the cost if they adopted enabling legislation to create Medicaid programs that met the conditions specified in the new federal law. These conditions included making the benefits available to all state residents who were eligible for welfare payments and including the entire list of services mandated by the law. States could also grant eligibility to the "medically needy" residents who met the other criteria but who had somewhat more income than permitted for welfare eligibility and who "spent down" enough of their income on covered medical expenses to effectively reduce it to that level. They also had the option of covering other services not included in the list of mandatory ones.

To achieve the public purpose of providing health care coverage to low-income people, the federal government offered to pay part of the cost. The federal share (called the federal medical assistance percentage, or FMAP) varied from 83 percent of state spending for the poorest states to as little as 50 percent of state spending for the richest states.

Some states passed enabling legislation pretty quickly, but others did not. The last state to create a Medicaid program was Arizona in 1982, seventeen years after passage of Title XIX.

By the time the ACA became law in 2010, not only did all states have Medicaid programs, these programs had become a critically important part of virtually all states' health care systems. As a result, if the program disappeared from a particular state, not only would many state residents no longer have financial access to needed services, providers in those states who treated large numbers of Medicaid-eligible residents would suddenly lose a substantial amount of revenue. Moreover, the hospitals among that group of providers are required by federal law to serve anyone who appears in their ED if they have one, at least to the point of stabilizing their conditions even if the patient cannot pay for his or her care.

So although Medicaid is voluntary for the states, the reality is that so many depend on it that they would have a hard time doing without it. As noted in Chapter Two, the ACA uses Medicaid as a major source of funds for expanding coverage to residents with incomes below 133 percent of the federal poverty line. Recognizing the additional financial burden this would impose on states, Congress agreed that, regardless of the state's FMAP, the federal government would pay 100 percent of the cost of the new people added to the Medicaid rolls until 2017 and then the federal share would fall gradually to 90 percent of the cost from 2020 onward. Along with that positive financial inducement, the ACA also includes a penalty for those states that nonetheless decide not to expand their Medicaid programs to accommodate all those additional beneficiaries. That penalty is to withhold the federal share for the state's entire Medicaid program.

In its decision upholding the constitutionality of the individual mandate, the Supreme Court also said the Medicaid penalty was unconstitutional because it amounted to coercion, and the federal government cannot force a state to accept a grant in aid like Medicaid. The positive inducement remains in place, but the penalty does not. The practical question thus becomes whether states will see the inducement as powerful enough to expand their Medicaid programs so that virtually all state residents will have health care coverage. Given the polarization in our politics, it is too early to predict what will happen. I will return to this question in Chapter Four.

THE PUBLIC POLICY CASE FOR THE ACA

Given the law's imperfections and the seriousness of the problems, it is not unreasonable to ask, despite the Court's decision, whether the ACA is the best we can do. Or, even if it is not, whether it is good enough to justify our support. Should we instead scrap it and try for something better? Not only did Mitt Romney, the Republican presidential candidate, promise he would "repeal Obamacare" if voters elected him president in 2012, but in the run up to passage in 2009 and early 2010, progressives too were having doubts about the wisdom of passage. The key issue for many of them was the failure of "the public option." This was a proposal to offer a publicly run insurance plan that would compete with the private plans that were to be made available through the state health exchanges. Proponents expected it to be fairer and less expensive and to do a better job keeping down costs than the private plans. They also thought it might evolve naturally into something like Medicare for All, which was the ultimate goal for many. Paul Starr writes that "the public-insurance option had taken on high symbolic importance for both the left and right, and in the final stages became the central focus of conflict in the Senate."[3] He added that "progressives . . . regarded it as a litmus test of worthwhile health-care reform, even though the idea had been drastically downgraded"[4] and had lost much of its real value as a policy alternative. The ACA's imperfections make legitimate these questions about whether the law deserves to be implemented. Indeed, they warrant serious consideration.

Let's begin by recognizing that, although the ACA addresses all the problems found in Chapter One, it does not tackle them in the most direct or straightforward way possible. And sometimes it does not take the strongest possible actions. Here are some examples:

- Instead of solving the access-to-coverage problem directly simply by making everyone eligible for a national health insurance program such as Medicare for All, the ACA requires that everyone buys coverage in the private market.

- Instead of creating a health insurance program with a comprehensive set of stated benefits, it establishes minimum content requirements for private insurance policies, charges the Secretary of Health and Human Services with defining the benefits in more detail, and assumes that the market will keep prices and other unspecified elements in line so that the law accomplishes its stated goals. As a result, it creates the need for extensive regulation to be certain that the private insurers really do provide access to comprehensive benefits for all Americans.

- Instead of changing the methods of paying providers in order to give them positive incentives to attack the spending and quality problems, the ACA constrains insurer behavior by making many of their most common cost-limiting tactics illegal. It thus creates a condition that makes it in the interest of individual insurers to negotiate new payment methods with their providers that change provider incentives so that they are more nearly aligned with the goals of the law. Since that is one of a very small number of options available to them, it is not unreasonable to expect insurers to do just that. On the other hand, provider organizations will need to respond with concerted actions on their part in order to influence individual clinicians to make different utilization choices that both improve quality of care and keep costs under control. (See the discussion of clinical decisions in Chapter One.) Since we have relatively little experience doing these things, the ultimate outcome is far from certain. I will have more to say about these issues in Chapter Four.

- Instead of creating a single program, which could dramatically reduce the administrative complexity that is an important contributor to cost inflation in the health sector, the ACA creates rules that can simplify some component system processes. These include consumers' choice among competing insurance plans, on the one hand, and claim submissions and payment processes, on the other. In other words, having chosen to rely on private markets to achieve key goals of reform, Congress did not assume, as a matter of faith, that markets will "automatically" achieve the goals of reform. Instead, the special health insurance markets ("exchanges") to be established in the states are charged with creating rules that, among other things, will facilitate consumers' ability to compare key features of competing policies.

Like many others, I begin with several convictions: (1) it is important for all to have real access to needed care; (2) costs need to be contained in order to protect both people's access to care and professionals' ability to deliver good quality care; and (3) the law contains important tools with which to make progress toward solving the problems and achieving the goals. In other words, the ACA's provisions add up to a multifront assault on health system problems with the potential to do much good for millions of individuals and for the country and the health system as a whole, but no guarantees.

Some might argue that the law was a cop-out; that it provides too little too late and that it does not and cannot really *solve* anything. Some of those folks may be partisans for a favorite strategy—like Medicare for All (single payer)—and may not see the value in other approaches that, while less robust perhaps, contain positive elements that can move us substantially ahead.

How far the law's provisions will actually take us and how close we will come to maximizing the potential will depend on decisions yet to be made—by insurers, employers, professional and institutional providers, citizens, and government officials at both federal and state levels.

It is important to recognize the fact that no reform can produce changes in how care is provided either immediately on a law's effective date or even with certainty over time. The only provisions that can create an immediate result are those that grant eligibility to all on a date certain for a single, publicly operated health insurance program—like Medicare for All. And even a single-payer program like that would only be a plan to *pay* for care. So while a new law could almost instantly transform us into a society with 100 percent access to coverage (like all the European countries), it is the nature of the beast that *all of the other reform goals— cost containment, improved reliability of care—will be achieved only over time, if at all.* And only after many individuals and organizations develop processes and implement plans that change their behavior to produce different and better utilization patterns (see Chapter One).

Here is an example of why that is true. To reduce the cost of actually providing care—not to mention to make the quality of care more reliable—will require that medical practices, hospitals, and other professionals and institutions change the clinical decisions they make and the way they organize and deliver services. Each practice will need to make choices and implement them, see the extent to which the changes produce positive results, and, if necessary, refine them. Moreover, for the impact to be large enough to affect the entire system to a measurable degree, *thousands of medical practices across the country* will need to do these things.

No legislation can create the desired results throughout the system immediately or even directly. Instead, what legislation *can* do is create conditions that encourage individuals and organizations with a variety of roles to play to act in desired ways. And over time, the sum total of those actions—if things work out as intended—will approximate the desired results. But even changing the incentives embedded in payment methods only creates opportunities. Some provider organizations will take advantage of them and transform themselves into more efficient practices that produce high-quality care more reliably than ever before. Other provider organizations will recognize the opportunity and try to make the most of it, but—perhaps because their managers are not as talented or their physicians are not as unified in their commitment to the changes—will fail to achieve the level of success of the first group. Still others may not be able to figure out what steps to take to improve, even if they would like to. And some may resist changing altogether.

The point is that many people must make many things happen before even a single group can actually improve its performance. And since we are aiming at nothing less than systemwide change, a very large percentage of practice organizations need not only to make the effort, but also to succeed at it before the changes bring down *national* health care expenditures or improve *national* health outcomes. Creating positive health system change is a daunting challenge—and passing the legislation, important and difficult as that was, was only the first step.

Add to this cautionary tale the fact that many cost reductions will result in less revenue to the medical practice that successfully introduces them. For them, therefore, a key question will be, How will they be able to survive financially with less income when even now they operate under such tremendous financial pressure? Improvements in efficiency may mean reducing duplicate services—for example, because an electronic medical record system avoids the problem of losing the results of recent tests—and providing fewer services (even if they are unnecessary) reduces income in a fee-for-service world. Decisions that produce benefits for patients and payers but reduce income for medical practices will only increase their financial burden, so those practices will need to come up with ways of lowering costs or increasing revenues. On that score, the addition of thirty-two million more people to the coverage rolls will help some medical practices that are able to attract a share of the newly insured. And figuring out ways to encourage already insured patients to use services differently—more preventive care, care earlier in an illness episode—can help, too. *The bottom line: change—even positive change—will take time.* No possible scenario can eliminate that fact. Therefore, even if a better law could be passed, one with more powerful tools for promoting change, the best that could be hoped for is that the change-producing process might be shortened somewhat. For these reasons, it is important to make the most of the opportunity created by the ACA.

THE POLITICAL CASE FOR THE ACA

Even if that were not the case, however, there is another reason—a compelling one, in my view—to try to make the Affordable Care Act work. Simply put, it is exceedingly unlikely that a better law could be passed any time soon. That is the inescapable conclusion from a review of the long history of prior reform efforts.

Almost every president from Franklin Roosevelt on has tried to reform the health care system. Some had more comprehensive plans than others, some were more committed to the effort than others, but as Blumenthal and Morone show in their book about the role of the president in health care reform, virtually all tried.[5] Yet, until Barack Obama's triumph with the Affordable Care Act, only Lyndon Johnson in 1965, using all the formidable skills developed during his years as leader of the Senate, had succeeded. Following the death of President Kennedy and the Democratic landslide in the 1964 election, he was able to persuade the Congress to adopt Titles XVIII and XIX of the Social Security Act, which created the Medicare and Medicaid programs. And, on the basis of information they uncovered at the Johnson Presidential Library, Blumenthal and Morone revealed that the conventional story, which for forty years gave most of the credit to House Ways and Means Committee Chair Wilbur Mills, was wrong. The reality is that it took all of the considerable abilities Johnson honed in his time as master of the Congress to get that law enacted even when political conditions were as auspicious as they were then.

So this prior history raises several questions of interest. Why is health care reform a perennial issue? Why has the struggle for national health insurance endured for so many decades? After so many defeats, why didn't its supporters simply give up? And, What changed so that the ACA passed in 2010?

Although the first proposals for national health insurance originated with Theodore Roosevelt in his 1912 campaign for the presidency, the first president actually to send a bill to Congress was Harry Truman in 1945–1946.[6] Morone describes the Truman proposal as "stillborn," but argues that it "produced two powerful ideas that would in turn influence future debates."[7]

The first idea was the social insurance principle, which holds that "a just and modern society takes care of people when they are sick. . . . Health care . . . was something we owed one another as fellow citizens."[8] Indeed, virtually every other developed country acted on that principle decades ago. But in the United States, when health care reform that includes universal coverage is proposed, it triggers "angry arguments against socialized medicine," which Morone reported "seem so wild, the rhetoric so exaggerated."[9]

Indeed, this scene played out repeatedly over the years. It is an illustration of what Hofstadter called the "paranoid style in American politics," which expressed itself as a "truculent fear of government." And each time it arose, Democrats who supported reform seemed "surprised by the ferocity of the opposition" because it was so divorced from reality. As Morone writes, whether or not national health insurance was good policy, "it was not really going to deliver America to the Soviets in the 1940s nor will it get up a bureaucratic panel to weigh grandpa's fate today."[10]

Because the issue represented a big hole in the social safety net that, among other things, was unique among modern industrial societies, it kept coming up. Yet the opposition was always able to beat it back. Why has passing health care reform been so difficult? As I wrote in *Still Broken*, many factors contributed to the failure of past reform efforts.[11] They include that paranoid "political culture" rooted in an "ambivalence toward government and . . . bias toward private solutions to public problems";[12] the absence of a strong labor movement; race, especially during the period prior to the 1960s when Southern Democrats dominated the Congress; and the structure of government, which gives veto power to even small numbers of opponents. The fact is that many different bodies—most important, the two houses of Congress—must agree to pass a major piece of legislation, but it takes only a few determined individuals to kill it.[13]

But while all these factors added to the difficulty, the underlying reason for the failure each time a reform attempt was made was the fact that either or both of two sets of interest groups proved to be too powerful for supporters of reform to overcome. Their arguments may have been overblown, as Morone asserts, but they were always able to keep the proposal from becoming law. One group had an economic stake in the health care system because they earned their livelihood from it. These were, especially, the doctors in the period up until the early 1960s and, in more recent years, the insurers. Other groups, too, including hospitals, as well as pharmaceutical firms and medical device manufacturers, have worked against reform. All benefited from the status quo and fought to maintain it. They contributed lots of money to the political campaigns of members of the House and Senate and cultivated relationships with those members with the goal of protecting their short-term financial interests. Over the years, they proved to be so successful that many draft bills never made it out of Congressional committees; in fact, in many cases it was impossible even to hold hearings or bring the bills to a committee vote.

Another main question is, Why was Barack Obama able to get a major reform law passed when strong-willed, skilled politicians such as Richard Nixon and Bill Clinton, among others, failed? What changed to allow the ACA to pass in 2010?

Beginning in the 1990s, during the Clinton reform episode, which occurred as the current period of hyperpartisanship began, another, non-economic interest group also demonstrated a determination to stymie reform efforts. That group consisted of Republican members of the House and Senate. The legislative process is, in the end, a competition for votes to enact laws. To succeed in passing particular legislative proposals, proponents try to create majorities by building coalitions of colleagues, which requires a willingness to compromise on the bills' provisions. Sometimes a member would agree to support a bill if a certain provision were deleted or changed or in exchange for a pledge from a colleague to support another bill to which the first member was committed. Why would members be willing to enter into compromises? In part, because they defined their jobs to be to find ways to solve the nation's problems through legislation.

In the period of the "tea party movement," however, many ideologically extreme members—mostly on the right end of the political spectrum—set their goals differently. They believe their definition of problems and their approach to solving them is the only appropriate way, and therefore they refuse to compromise with members who have different perspectives on the issues. Convinced of the rightness of their positions, they expect to win in the end if they can just hold out and resist the temptation to collaborate with members on the other side of the aisle. In her book about the Clinton health care reform episode, the Harvard political scientist Theda Skocpol shared a memo she discovered that warned Republican members against compromise because that would give President Clinton a triumph and delay the otherwise inevitable victory of their side.[14] Fast forward to 2009, the year Barack Obama was sworn in as president, and Senator Mitch McConnell of Kentucky, the Republican leader in the Senate, said for all to hear that his number one goal was to make sure that Barack Obama was a one-term president. Throughout virtually President Obama's entire first term (that is, at this writing in the fall of 2012), Republicans have almost never compromised on any important legislation.

So, against these odds, the fact that President Obama, House Speaker Nancy Pelosi, and Senate Majority Leader Harry Reid were able to pass the Patient Protection and Affordable Care Act was a monumental accomplishment. How did they do it?[15]

To oversimplify: in a difficult environment characterized by extraordinary deficits, the worst fiscal crisis since the Depression, and a toxic hyperpartisan atmosphere, the administration based important elements of its strategy on lessons learned from prior episodes, especially the Clinton-era attempt from the mid-1990s.

For example, the administration got started early in the term. Indeed, the president overruled advisers who, knowing the history of prior reform efforts, opposed expending any of his political capital on such a difficult, if not hopeless, undertaking. He "pressed to get the reform passed in his first year . . . and repeatedly set deadlines for Congress."[16]

Further, instead of demonizing insurers and providers and other health system stakeholders, the Obama administration "sought to neutralize any stakeholder opposition."[17] Implicitly, the president acknowledged that the "worsening state of American health insurance . . . did have very particular costs for key stakeholders in the medical industry."[18] That being the case, apart from the obvious political value of doing so, he recognized that it was reasonable to expect those stakeholders, even if they were willing to contemplate a reformed system, to want to protect their interests or at least to minimize the short-term price they would pay.

So, for example, by basing the strategy on reforming the private health insurance system and then expanding it to achieve close to universal coverage, Obama gave insurers an opportunity to benefit from the reforms even if the public and the system itself would benefit more. As we saw in Chapter Two, some of those insurance reforms imposed serious constraints on private insurers' ability to maximize their profits, but the prospect of as many as thirty-two million new subscribers was seen as enough of a benefit to allow them to accept the reforms.

Further, instead of presenting the Congress with a detailed blueprint for reform, as Bill Clinton had done, Barack Obama enunciated some principles and left it to Congress to work out the details. Thus, instead of outlining "a grand theory of reform and a vision of transforming the delivery system through managed competition," as the Clinton administration had done, the Obama administration pushed "incremental, friendly-sounding reforms such as electronic health records, prevention, and medical homes."[19] That approach gave Congressional leaders the opportunity, at least, to put their own stamp on the legislation. Moreover, involving the Congress so deeply apparently paid another crucial dividend when negotiations threatened to break down in the early winter of 2009–2010. As the end approached and the bargaining got tougher, some in the administration wanted to pull back and some Democratic members of Congress wanted to pass a series of smaller bills, each of which would enact a popular provision, instead of going for one big reform package. But some of the senators who had been most involved in the tough bargaining process argued they had invested too much of themselves and were "too close to the finish line" to give up on a comprehensive reform bill.[20] Of import, the president himself "chose to go for broke."[21] He realized they were closer than most of his predecessors had come and, thinking he could see a potential path to victory, the alternative of settling for "minor incremental policies" was unappealing because it would mean that the entire daunting process would need to play out again at some future time.

Mark Peterson, the UCLA political scientist, argues that a key reason that the process got to the brink of passage was that this "period of health care reform [was] so different from past episodes."[22] In particular, "only during Bill Clinton's administration did the scope and urgency of the policy problems, a potential driver of reform, come close to matching those of the current period."[23] He asserts that "[g]overnment is not likely to act unless there are fairly strong perceptions—among the public or at least among state actors—that problems amendable [sic] to public-sector intervention actually exist."[24] The first two years of President Obama's administration saw a combined policy-problem, institutional, and political context that was more "favorable to health care reform" than at any previous period. But as the Clinton experience demonstrated, the presence of a favorable context is no guarantee of action. Another key ingredient is presidential leadership, and this president demonstrated throughout the long process the seriousness of his commitment to health care reform.

The problems were serious, conditions were favorable, and early in his first term the president, who was committed to reform, set in motion the long and difficult legislative process summarized in the last few pages. Nonetheless, the negotiations dragged on month after month, and until the deal was finally reached, there was no certainty that a bill would in fact pass. In the Senate, a group of moderate Democratic senators, led by Max Baucus of Montana, tried to work out a bipartisan plan with moderate Republican colleagues, led by Senator Charles Grassley of Iowa. In addition, three House committees worked on separate bills until the speaker, Nancy Pelosi, pushed them to come up with a single House version, which she was able to pass in the fall of 2009. Finally, the Senate passed a version, too, just before Christmas, with absolutely no Republican support—despite all those months of meetings. The two bills seemed to set the scene for the traditional process under which House and Senate conferees would come up with a single compromise bill that substituted some provisions of one House's version for provisions in the other. Since both Houses were controlled by Democrats and each one had passed a bill, though not a slam dunk, it appeared that a reform law might actually come to pass just after the first of the year.

But then the voters in liberal Massachusetts of all places threw a monkey wrench into the process and, in a special election on January 19, 2010, to fill the seat of the late Senator Ted Kennedy, who had died the previous summer, chose Republican state senator Scott Brown over the heavily favored Democratic attorney general Martha Coakley. Perhaps because she was overconfident, she ran a lackluster campaign against the largely unknown, but charming Scott Brown. The immediate effect of Brown's election was to deprive Democrats in the Senate of the sixty-vote super majority they needed to avoid a Senate filibuster, reconcile the House and Senate versions of health sector reform, and come up with a new bill that combined parts of the two original bills. To cope with the new situation, Harry Reid and Nancy Pelosi engineered a plan under which the House adopted the Senate version with the promise that the Senate, using the budget reconciliation process, which required only a simple majority of fifty-one votes, would then pass a companion bill that included changes in the Senate's version that Democratic House members wanted. The new situation also gave considerable leverage to several Democratic senators on the more conservative end of the political spectrum,[25] which they used to extract concessions that would benefit their home states and, they hoped, protect them from in-state opposition during their own 2010 reelection campaigns.

At the eleventh hour, the Senate did pass such a bill, and the House adopted it, as well. And so the Patient Protection and Affordable Care Act became law when President Obama signed it on March 23, 2010.

CONCLUSION

So here is my answer to the questions posed at the beginning of this chapter: Was it a good idea to pass the law? Should it be overturned?

Yes, it was a good idea to pass the ACA, and no, it should not be overturned.

The problems facing the U.S. health care system are serious. The ACA may not be ideal, but it makes available valuable tools for creating substantial progress on achieving the goals of better access to care, cost containment, and more reliable quality of care. If the law had been scrapped because, in the 2012 election, Republicans had won both the presidency and majorities in both houses of the Congress and were able to muster the votes to repeal it, passage of a substitute bill—whether better or not—would have been exceedingly unlikely.

For these reasons, the rational choice is to make the best of the ACA. Having said that, the results actually achieved will depend on decisions to be made by many—with different roles to play, a variety of interests in the outcomes, and uncertain capacity to create positive change. In Chapter Four, we turn to four of the big challenges to be faced:

- The use of Medicaid to pay for a large part of the expansion of health insurance
- The importance of implementation of the law's provisions as illustrated by the battle over the Medical Loss Ratio
- The creation of health insurance exchanges
- The creation of positive changes to the delivery of care as illustrated by a new set of organizations, accountable care organizations (ACOs).

4 MAKING CHANGE

The most useful way to see the Affordable Care Act is as a law that provides a variety of tools, incentives, and grants that create opportunities for public officials and others to accomplish many good things both for the health system as a whole and for individual Americans who depend on and use that system. The corollary is that what is actually accomplished under the law depends on how well those opportunities are used.

The people who will have the largest roles in determining the actual accomplishments include the following:

- Federal civil servants and others in the executive branch who will create and then enforce the regulations required to implement the law.

- The Congress, which, through its power over the purse, can fund the new law adequately or starve it so that its promise cannot be realized.

- State officials who will create the health insurance exchanges (or not), regulate insurance plans, and operate the Medicaid program, among other things.

- Clinicians and other leaders of health care delivery organizations. For the law to lead to more reliable quality and to contain expenditures will require above all that doctors and other clinical professionals make different—that is, better— clinical decisions that produce more salutary patient utilization patterns. In other words, it is up to them to create improved care-giving processes that produce more reliable quality of care, fewer medical errors, fewer unnecessary and duplicate services, and reduced costs. To generate those results will require the leaders of health care delivery organizations— from one- or two-person medical offices to multispecialty group practices, hospitals, and other large organizations—to develop and implement new policies and practices that accomplish those goals.

- Individuals who (1) obtain comprehensive health insurance (many will simply retain the policies they already have) and (2) use health care services differently than they do at present to produce new and more effective aggregate utilization patterns.

Getting Congress to pass the ACA was a monumental legislative accomplishment. Making sure that the new law lives up to its promise shifts the focus to implementation. In part, that means detailed work by career officials in federal and state governments over a period of several years. As Rogan Kersh put it, "Implementing the Affordable Care Act will take years . . . and involves a mountain of intricately specified new regulations. Even apparently simple sections require extensive elaboration."[1] The paragraph in the law providing that children could remain on their parents' health insurance until age twenty-six generated "more than two dozen pages of regulatory details in the *Federal Register*."[2]

But implementation is more than technical work by anonymous bureaucrats. "Virtually every provision in the ACA provides a fresh political battlefield, training a spotlight on regulators accustomed to laboring in relative privacy."[3] And that means more politics, because the fact is that parties with many different interests have important roles to play under the new law or will be affected by it. And it is only natural to expect that they will act to protect their interests.

Although the process contains many opportunities for delay and even gridlock, the good news is that "the rule-making process has proceeded largely on schedule. . . . In fact, [n]umerous deadlines . . . have been shifted earlier, often by months."[4] Things may slow down as the work continues, but as of November 2012, there is reason for optimism.

In this chapter we will look at four examples that will illustrate the opportunities and the challenges that will be faced by these individuals. If they succeed in seizing the opportunities and overcoming the challenges, the U.S. health care system will be much closer to the ideal all would like to see. Ultimately, success will be determined by individuals and the extent to which they have both the commitment and the skill to make these good things happen. To some degree that will mean their recognizing the incentives and opportunities available in the law and regulations and taking advantage of them. For some, it will also mean being able to withstand external pressure from interest groups and influential others (that is, lobbyists, elected Congressional representatives, and political appointees) that would promote the short-term interests of those groups instead of the longer-term public interest.

MEDICAID—A KEY VEHICLE FOR EXPANDING COVERAGE

We saw in Chapter Two that a big part of the strategy to increase the number of insured Americans was to require the states to expand their Medicaid programs to include everyone under age sixty-five with incomes up to 133 percent of the federal poverty level. Instead of the usual federal medical assistance percentage (FMAP), however, the federal government would pay 100 percent of the cost of people added to a state's Medicaid rolls as a result of ACA provisions, from 2014, when this part of the law becomes effective, through 2016, after which the federal share would be reduced gradually until it settles at 90 percent by 2020.

The federal share of the additional cost was portrayed as an inducement to the states to adopt these provisions. But in addition to that carrot, the law also contained a stick: states that refused to go along with this provision would lose the entire federal share of the state's total Medicaid spending. The administration saw this as part of the inducement to states to sign on to the plan. As we saw in Chapter Three, however, the Supreme Court by a vote of 7-2 ruled that it was coercion, which is unconstitutional and therefore not permitted. Since the federal government cannot *require* states to adopt such programs, it has long been established that they can make it so attractive that states voluntarily agree to do so. But since Medicaid is an established program on which state governments, medical care providers, and low-income eligibles depend, the states *need* federal matching funds. Thus, since they cannot refuse the federal matching money associated with the rest of their Medicaid program, the Court decided they were being *forced* to expand it to accommodate the new eligibles.

The effect of this ruling was to make Medicaid expansion an option for the states instead of a requirement. How many of the states will now refuse to participate in the Medicaid expansion? How many will expand the program to some, but not all of those who otherwise would be eligible? And of those, what would the nature and amount of the expansion be? The answers to these questions will determine how close the United States comes to having 100 percent of the population with health insurance.

Although it may have been necessary politically to secure passage of the ACA, from a policy perspective, relying on Medicaid as a key element to meet the coverage-expansion goals creates a number of potential problems. The fact that individual state governments will be making key policy decisions regarding eligibility and other matters undermines the goal of creating a single national program. Residents of one state may have a different experience than similarly situated residents of other states. Moreover, since states now have the ability to opt out of the program altogether, it is possible that low-income residents of some states will not have a way to gain eligibility for the program at all.

Although the underlying Medicaid programs, which now exist in all states, were created under provisions of a federal law, Title XIX of the Social Security Act, they vary considerably one from another. That is because, in contrast to Title XVIII, which created a single federal Medicare program for the elderly (later amended to include the chronically ill and those with end stage renal disease), the Medicaid Title gave states considerable decision-making discretion. They could make key programmatic decisions related to eligibility criteria; the amount, duration, and scope of covered benefits; and payment rates for ambulatory service providers.

Among other things, eligibility criteria vary from state to state. Table 4.1 illustrates the differences. It reports data for two relatively poor southern states and two of the largest, richest, and most generous states, as well as the lowest and highest state measures and

TABLE 4.1.
Medicaid data for selected states

	A. Income Eligibility Levels, 2011–2012 (% FPL)		B. Medicaid Payments Per Enrollee, FY 2009 ($)
	Children	Working Parents	
Alabama	300	24	4,081
Mississippi	200	44	4,890
New York	400	150	8,960
California	250	106	3,527
Highest	400	215	9,577
Lowest	160	24	3,527
United States	250	63	5,527

SOURCES: Kaiser Commission on Medicaid and the Uninsured, *Why Does Medicaid Spending Vary Across States? A Chart Book of Factors Driving State Spending*, October 2012. Column A, Table 4a, page 22; Column B, Summary Table, page 5.

the U.S. total. It shows that children in Alabama are eligible for Medicaid up to 300 percent of the poverty line while those in Mississippi, another poor, Southern state, are eligible only up to 200 percent of the poverty line. Similarly, New York and California vary between 250 percent and 400 percent of poverty. New York's eligibility for children is the highest in the nation; the lowest is 160 percent of poverty. The interstate variation is similar for working parents, a less favored group, except at much lower levels of income.

Not only do eligibility criteria differ across the states, but so do the amount of payments per enrollee. Again, Alabama and Mississippi are on the low end of the scale, while New York is among the highest. Interestingly, California spends even less on average per enrollee than the two southern states.

What accounts for these differences? The answer is complex, but one factor undoubtedly is the relative wealth of the states. Alabama and Mississippi are just poorer than California and New York. So even if Alabama and Mississippi policymakers were inclined to be as generous as their counterparts in New York and California, they may not have the funds to support such a decision. One measure of state fiscal capacity is per capita personal income, as shown in Table 4.2.

New York's and California's annual per capita income for 2011 was $13,000 to $16,000 higher than those in Alabama and Mississippi. And per capita income was more than $22,000 higher in the highest state than in New York. The average across all states was more than $39,000. Indeed, the large variation in state wealth is one of the important reasons why we have national or federal programs instead of relying entirely on the states to serve these purposes. Wealthier states tend to subsidize poorer states so that residents of the nation as a whole can attain a satisfactory level of access to characteristics that define modern industrial societies—not just health care but also education, paved roads, and other services and elements of infrastructure. Moreover, while some states appear to be permanently better off than some others, the identities of the states

TABLE 4.2.

Selected state data

	A. Personal Income Per Capita 2011 ($)	B. State Tax Revenue, SFY 2010 ($ millions)	C. Percentage of State Revenues (all sources) to Medicaid, FY 2009–2011	D. Health Care Expenditures Per Capita, 2009 ($)
Alabama	33,411	8.2	25.8	6,272
Mississippi	30,401	6.3	22.9	6,571
New York	46,516	63.5	28.7	8,341
California	42,395	104.8	18.9	6,238
Highest	68,843	104.8	34.4	10,349
Lowest	30,401	1.3	7.3	5,031
United States	39,635	702.2	22.3	6,815

SOURCES: Kaiser Commission on Medicaid and the Uninsured. *Why Does Medicaid Spending Vary Across States? A Chart Book of Factors Driving State Spending*, October 2012. Column A, Table 1a, page 9; Column B, Appendix Table 1, page 42; Column C, Appendix Table 2, page 43; Column D, Table 3a, page 17.

in the well-off and weaker groups vary from time to time so that state A may be a net subsidizer one year and state B a beneficiary of that largesse, while five years later, the reverse may be the case. Think about the decline of the once-thriving "rust belt" states, whose manufacturing industries were once a powerful engine of America's vaunted economic success but have been in the midst of a long-term decline.

A related factor is the state's capacity to pay the state share of Medicaid expenditures. Table 4.2 shows differences in state tax revenues and the proportion of state revenues that are used for Medicaid. Again, these numbers vary considerably. States' tax revenues are a function of both tax rates and state wealth. So poorer states have less capacity to tax themselves and produce the revenues needed to run a program such as Medicaid. If that lesser wealth coexists with a view that the public sector should be small and serve only limited functions, they may also choose to tax themselves at lower rates, as well. This combination of factors limits the amount of money states have available to spend on Medicaid.

Another factor that contributes to the interstate differences is comparative state attitudes toward the poor and toward public-sector responsibility for a variety of services. Many of these attitudes can be traced back even to colonial times. To oversimplify, colonial New England tended to be characterized by small farms and small towns organized around a common. Living independently but in proximity to one another, residents developed methods and structures for taking care of one another when the need arose. Government was often embodied in the iconic New England town meeting. As small New England towns grew into much larger nineteenth-century cities, with growing numbers of people packed into smaller spaces, that tendency increased. City and state governments grew and took on more and more responsibilities.

The south remained a largely agricultural society for much longer than the north. Farmers took a more paternalistic attitude toward their workers, many of whom were slaves until the mid-nineteenth century. County governments with their populations more widely dispersed over a larger geographic area were more important in the south than in the north. Partly because they decided they did not need to do so, they did not take on all the functions that northern cities absorbed.

I can illustrate how the differences play out in relation to Medicaid. All states need to watch their spending on this program because it, like other programs that pay for health care, grows simply because of the way care is delivered and paid for. But southern states and northern states have developed characteristically different ways of trying to keep down their spending. In the south, it tends to be harder to become eligible for Medicaid and other public-sector programs, but providers of services tend to be paid at rates closer to the higher rates paid by Medicare than in the north. Eligibility criteria tend to be lower in the north so that more people can become eligible for benefits, but providers of care tend to be paid less.

Finally, another of the factors affecting Medicaid spending is that medical care costs more in some states than in others. Column D in Table 4.2 shows differences in state-level per capita health spending (not limited to Medicaid). While spending is influenced by the incidence of illness and the availability of services, variations in the cost of living, including the cost of medical care, also contribute to differences in Medicaid spending.

These differences in state Medicaid programs produce different results, as well, and those differences will have an effect on the extent to which the ACA actually meets its coverage expansion goals. States vary in the percentage of their populations who are currently uninsured and eligible for Medicaid.[5] And they also vary in the extent to which currently eligible adults actually enroll in the program.[6] It turns out that those states which do a poorer job of actually enrolling Medicaid-eligible adults tend on average to be among the poorer states even though the need arguably is greater. And they also have a larger proportion of adults who will become eligible for Medicaid in 2014 when the coverage-expanding provisions of the ACA go into effect. So if they fully adopt the Medicaid provisions, they will have proportionally more people to enroll. Fortunately, the federal government will pick up 100 percent of the tab for those newly eligible people who enroll—but not, it turns out, for those who were already eligible but had not enrolled. To the extent that a state's program expands by adding such people to the rolls, the federal government will pay only the regular FMAP, which varies from 50 percent to 83 percent of state spending.

Given these interstate differences, it is not surprising that the part of the ACA that uses Medicaid as the vehicle to expand health insurance coverage for low-income Americans gives states considerable flexibility in implementing Medicaid-related provisions of the ACA. That flexibility is needed because the states are starting at such different places, not only in regard to eligibility, benefits, and payments, but also in relation to administration.

Here is just one example: "The ACA envisions that states will create coordinated integrated eligibility and enrollment systems for Medicaid, Children's Health Insurance Program (CHIP), and exchange coverage that will, in most cases, provide real-time eligibility determinations and rely on electronic data exchanges to the greatest extent possible."[7] One reason is that eligibility for benefits for many people is expected to migrate between the state health insurance exchange and the state Medicaid program as they move into and out of the workforce. That means that providers wanting to check on the coverage of the patient sitting in the waiting room need to be able to access real-time eligibility information. Yet while some states "have made significant progress in achieving real-time eligibility determination, other electronic simplification, and in coordinating Medicaid and CHIP enrollment, . . . many other states continue to rely on outdated paper-based eligibility systems."[8]

Federal officials will also be monitoring the experience under the ACA as it unfolds across the country. They will develop a series of measures designed to capture progress regarding eligibility, enrollment, utilization of services, and spending. Another implication of interstate differences is that some states will not be able easily to produce evidence of their system's performance. As a result, the set of measures that ultimately will be adopted will need to reflect differences in state data-producing capacity. These may evolve over time as state systems improve, but at the start, it is likely that some states will have an easier time showing their accomplishments than others.[9]

The bottom line regarding reliance on Medicaid as an important component of the effort to expand coverage is that it makes achieving stable, uniform national coverage much more difficult. The reasons are that states make key decisions, their Medicaid and other public-sector programs start from different points, they have different attitudes toward public-sector involvement in the social safety net and other elements of the health care system as well as in the economy in general, and they have different capacity to invest in expanding their Medicaid programs and upgrading their related administrative capabilities. Moreover, political and economic interests at the state level will attempt to influence state-level policies for their benefit, and we know from experience that when the public's interest differs from theirs, it often loses out in those struggles. Nonetheless, more Americans will gain health insurance coverage through state Medicaid programs, and we will make progress toward achieving the goal of universal coverage. To a considerable extent, however, it will be up to the federal government to ensure that the states' implementation of the new law is faithful to the framers' intent. That story will be written over the next five to ten years.

REGULATIONS—THE MEDICAL LOSS RATIO

The Affordable Care Act limits the proportion of premium income that private health insurers can spend on activities that do not contribute to patient health—that is, on things such as administration, marketing and promotion, executive compensation, and profits. Those offering health insurance policies to individuals and small businesses (firms with one hundred or fewer employees) must spend at least 80 percent of their premium income on health care claims and quality improvement; large-group insurers must spend at least 85 percent on those functions. Since insurers consider the money they spend on medical care to be a loss, the 80 percent and 85 percent figures are referred to as the medical loss ratio (MLR). When insurers spend less than those amounts, the ACA requires them to refund money to their customers. The Department of Health and Human Services reported that in 2012, about 12.8 million people will receive rebates totaling about $1.1 billion.[10]

Why would the law include these provisions? The reason is that, according to the evidence, many insurers spent less than those amounts on medical care and, as a result, Congress was concerned that prior to the ACA consumers were not getting—and more important, would not get under the new law—good value for their premium dollars. To illustrate, in 2010, investor-owned health insurers spent an *average* of only 81 percent of premiums on medical care. That represents a dramatic reduction from 1993 when the comparable figure was 95 percent of premiums.[11] Also in 2010, only 43 percent of "credible insurers"[12] in the individual market met MLR standards: 70 percent in the small-group market; and 77 percent in the large-group market.[13] What these numbers mean is that many Americans have not been getting good coverage from the health insurance they bought. The minimum MLR requirements were intended to make sure that in the future, everyone does.

Given ACA goals and pre-ACA circumstances, the MLR provisions of the law do not seem unreasonable. But they create a challenge for regulators: besides the bills for specific health care services actually delivered to patients, regulators must define exactly what expenses can fairly be said to improve quality of care? One of the regulators' tasks, therefore, is to spell out what activities can be considered to improve quality. Health insurance is a pretty complicated enterprise, and writing rules like this requires expertise. To provide such expertise that, at the same time, is oriented toward protecting the public interest, Congress specified in the legislation that the National Association of Insurance Commissioners (NAIC) be asked to draft regulations for the Secretary of Health and Human Services (HHS) to review and then, hopefully, approve.

What is the NAIC? Was it a good choice to take on that role? "The NAIC is a private, nonprofit organization that has coordinated the activities of the nation's state and territorial insurance commissioners since 1871. Its members are the insurance commissioners of the states and territories."[14] Timothy Jost identifies several reasons that the NAIC was given implementation responsibilities under the ACA. First, it asked for a role, arguing to Congress that "its open and transparent model-law development process was the most consumer-friendly approach for implementing [the new law and was even] . . . superior to the HHS rulemaking process."[15] Second, given that the law contemplates a large role for the states, it is a natural partner since its membership includes all state insurance commissioners and it has a long history of consulting individual states and drawing on the expertise of state-level technical staff. Third, it has considerable technical expertise on the complex insurance-related issues that need to be resolved. Given this, it is a more-than credible alternative to the expertise of the private insurers' own staffs, thus providing a way to avoid the obvious bias they would bring to the task. Indeed, in the absence of NAIC-like organizations, other federal agencies do often rely on "the technical competence of private organizations to shape and implement regulatory policy"[16] and therefore give rise to the concept of "regulatory capture" by the very groups intended to be regulated. Finally, the NAIC has an "unusually open and participatory administrative process" that not only invites consumer participation but pays the expenses that allow many of them to take part actively. In the case of the ACA, "eighteen funded consumer representatives were chosen, seventeen of whom were able to serve for the entire year."[17] Moreover, ten additional consumer representatives, representing national disease and consumer advocacy organizations that could afford to cover their expenses, served as unfunded consumer representatives."[18]

The NAIC process includes the creation of a "drafting subgroup, composed of technical staff drawn from several state insurance departments"[19] to prepare proposals on the various issues. The process is opened up by circulating those drafts to "interested parties" that have registered to participate. Much of the remaining work then occurs during long conference calls to discuss the proposals, followed by written comments submitted by some of the participants and then still further discussions. Eventually a revised and refined proposal "will be voted on by the NAIC Executive Committee and the 'Plenary,' the full body of all commissioners."[20]

In the end, the NAIC-orchestrated process, by all accounts, resulted in a fair and sensible set of rules defining the medical loss ratio. It is easy to imagine that a different process dominated by the insurers might have produced results that were less favorable to the general public and tilted more to insurer interests. Indeed, the academic literature on regulation is full of stories of such outcomes.[21]

Senator Jay Rockefeller of West Virginia described the challenge in a letter to Jane L. Cline, the West Virginia insurance commissioner who, at the time, was president of the NAIC. He wrote that the "new law allows health insurance companies to add their quality improvement expenditures to their incurred claims to calculate their medical loss ratios."[22] The law created this new category "to encourage health insurance companies to spend money on health care services that have been demonstrated to improve the safety, timeliness, and effectiveness of the care patients receive." Since the ACA limits the MLR to 80 percent of premiums for plans in the individual and small-group market and to 85 percent in the large-group market, "health insurance companies have a strong financial incentive to reclassify as many administrative and business functions as possible as 'quality-improving' expenditures in order to avoid paying rebates" to customers.[23] Indeed, according to Senator Rockefeller, the industry proposed that "almost any expenditure health insurers make in the normal course of their business is intended to improve the quality" of their policyholders' care.[24] According to Senator Rockefeller, among the expenses they claimed improved quality were the following: "The money health insurance companies

- spend processing and paying claims;
- spend creating and maintaining their provider networks;
- spend updating their information technology systems to code medical conditions and process claims payments; and
- use to conduct 'utilization review' of paid claims to detect payments the companies deem inappropriate and retroactively deny them."[25]

The subgroup that considered these proposals rejected them and instead defined quality-improvement expenses as those that actually "advance the delivery of patient-centered care" and that should be "capable of being objectively measured."[26]

Eventually, the NAIC process produced rules that rejected almost all of the insurers' proposals, and as a result, the MLR provision will serve the public interest as Congress intended in the ACA.

Although the experience of developing regulations related to the medical loss ratio turned out well for the general public, many other regulations are being developed—at the federal level and in all fifty states—to guide the implementation of other provisions. Organized stakeholders will attempt to influence the regulation writers, as the insurers did in the MLR example, to tweak the rules in ways that will benefit them. Given prior experience, it is likely that many will succeed, including perhaps some relating to the innovations discussed in the next two sections.

HEALTH INSURANCE EXCHANGES

The ACA requires almost everyone to obtain health insurance. For most adults under age sixty-five and their families, that will mean getting coverage through their employment, as has been the case for many years. Some, however, will be unable to get insurance through that route for one of several reasons: their employers don't offer plans, the plans offered by their employers are too expensive, or the individuals are self-employed, unemployed, or retired but younger than age sixty-five. For those people, instead of leaving them to fend for themselves in a brutal, expensive health insurance market dominated now by for-profit firms, the ACA requires that each state create a "health insurance exchange" (HIX) for the purpose of organizing a health insurance market in a way that facilitates individuals' ability to purchase coverage that conforms to requirements in the law. Among other things, they are intended to bring many of the benefits available to employees of large employers, especially choice among plans and lower premiums that result from both larger, more diverse risk pools and negotiation between employer and insurer. The expected result is that individuals in these markets will be able to obtain better insurance at lower prices than in the pre-ACA individual and small-group markets. The HIX are to be operational by January 1, 2014. To ensure they will be ready by the due date, the federal government can intervene before then in those states that fail to meet certain milestones.

Remember that all health insurance policies must cover at minimum a standard benefit package, that the premiums are to be set on a community-rated basis, that policies can offer only four levels of cost-sharing, and that individuals and families that qualify are entitled to subsidies to help them pay for the required coverage. Moreover, if the market in a state is an active one, individuals will need to be able to compare available policies in order to make a rational choice among those that are available. The HIX are intended to ensure that all these features are present and operating effectively in a particular state (or in a group of states that combine for the purpose of creating a single multistate market). Finally, if a particular state government decides not to create an HIX or if the federal government determines its exchange is not capable of performing the functions adequately, the federal government may step in to create the exchange itself. In other words, to a large extent, it is the HIX that is expected to enforce the law's provisions.

Since lots of money will be at stake, it can be expected that health insurers and other stakeholders in each state will try to influence the decisions that will result in a functioning HIX. So again, we are likely to see politics on display during this part of the implementation phase too.

In this section, we will discuss the legislative provisions intended to guide these activities and the implementation challenges they present.

The Purposes of Health Insurance Exchanges[27]

Let's start with understanding the principal purposes the health insurance exchanges are supposed to play. At the most basic level, the exchanges are intended to organize the sale of health insurance that meets the conditions of the law for those residents in the small-group and individual markets to purchase. They will not affect most people who obtain insurance from large employers. The main exception will be those individuals for whom their employers' offerings are too expensive.

What does it mean to organize the sale of health insurance? Simply put, it means qualifying a group of firms and their offerings and arranging to present them to individuals in the market in a way that makes clear the differences among them in benefits, available providers, and cost. They will also play a role in determining eligibility for the low-income subsidies the law makes available so that everyone is able to purchase conforming insurance.

A state may create a single exchange for both individual and small-group markets or a separate one for each, it may also join with neighboring states to form a regional exchange for one or both such markets, and a large state with several distinct health care markets may create more than one substate exchange. Each exchange must put in place a set of criteria that insurers wanting to offer plans to qualified residents must meet. They will include

- A minimum benefit package
- No more than four levels of cost-sharing (at 40 percent, 30 percent, 20 percent, and 10 percent levels)
- Premiums set on a modified community-rating basis (adjusted only for family size, age, geography, and whether or not the family contains smokers)
- Information on key provisions in a common format to facilitate consumer choice among available offerings.

In addition to these functions, the exchange must enforce provisions that all insurers—those in the individual and small-group markets, which are their main concern, as well as the large-employer market—must adopt. These include the prohibition against preexisting condition exclusions for children and later for adults as well; prohibitions against annual and lifetime benefit caps; prohibitions against rescissions; and individual and small-group insurer spending of at least 80 percent of premiums on approved medical care and quality improvement activities (the medical loss ratio).

To perform these functions, an exchange must have a budget that is adequate and a professional staff who are capable of performing them, although it is possible that an exchange might decide to purchase some of the services from vendors (such as the creation of a website that arrays in user-friendly fashion all relevant information for small businesses and individual consumers). In that case, it would need a process for issuing requests for proposals, for selecting among competing bids, and then for monitoring vendor performance.

Regarding *benefits*, the floor will be provided in the Act and by regulation of the Secretary of HHS. Then the exchange will need to decide whether to specify a set of uniform benefits at each cost-sharing tier or to allow actuarial equivalence among offered plans. Too much choice can be confusing to consumers and potentially can lead to adverse selection; too little can stifle the innovation that competition is supposed to foster.

Although cost-sharing at the level of 30 percent or 40 percent of the cost of services used will cause hardship for many in these markets—in my opinion, this is an unfortunate weakness in the law from the consuming public's point of view—the advantages of limiting them to four levels are to simplify decision making for consumers and to reduce the potential for biased risk selection.

Community rating means that premiums are set in advance for the entire group of people who will choose policies at any of the four levels of cost sharing. The alternative would be for the insurer to price policies separately for each potential purchaser on the basis of that person's or family's own health-related characteristics (called "experience rating"). The point is the same whether the individual is buying insurance in a separate individual market or through a small employer. Among other things, it greatly simplifies the insurer's functions and thus should reduce its costs. It also simplifies matters for the potential buyers—whether small businesses choosing offerings for their employees or the employees themselves—who, after all, would have no leverage on their own in dealing with an insurer that was pricing policies individually. Potentially, such an insurer could set the experience-rated price so high as to discourage a high-risk individual from buying its policy and thus avoid exposure to potentially high utilization costs. From the consumer's perspective, then, community rating is a good thing.

All these functions are intended to occur in a new market for individual and small-group consumers of health insurance. Therefore, the fundamental function for each HIX is to create a market in which, at base, insurers are willing to participate by offering policies to individuals and small groups. The theory, after all, is that competition among insurers will stimulate innovation and efficiency and permit competitors to offer low prices that are appealing to consumers.[28] The HIX must balance its role as facilitator for individuals and small groups wanting insurance with its role as creator of a market in which insurers are willing to participate. Undoubtedly, some insurers will decide they are not strong enough to compete in new markets like these in which utilization rates are uncertain (despite efforts to establish premiums that are fair to both consumers and insurers). Others will want as much flexibility as possible to tailor their offerings in ways that will reduce their risk and maximize their opportunities for profit. The challenges for the HIX are twofold: establishing rules and criteria that create a market that offers real choice to the state's residents and then monitoring the insurers' performance and enforcing those rules. Among other things, people buying insurance expect services provided by doctors, hospitals, and other professional clinicians to be paid for under the terms of a particular policy. In the pre-ACA days, one of the principal complaints was that insured patients used services and clinicians provided them in good faith to patients with coverage only to discover after the fact that, for one reason or another, the bill did not get paid. That is one of the eventualities the new law is expected to avoid.

Implementation Challenges

By any fair reading, the health exchanges have their work cut out for them, especially in the beginning before they develop a history of experience and can settle into a maintenance-of-successful-effort mode. One of the first decisions a state's legislature must make is how to organize its exchange. Should it be a department of state government (a new function for the insurance department is one example)? Alternatively, should it be a semi-independent authority governed by a board of directors appointed by the governor? The legislation creating the board would specify criteria for choosing the board's members, ensuring that they have relevant experience and at the same time represent a broad political spectrum (to strengthen its legitimacy and ongoing support). In that case, it will be important that consumer representatives on the board have sufficient numbers and expertise to be effective in protecting the interests of consumers. Whatever choice is made, the entity must be held politically accountable for performing all its functions, including attracting insurers willing to compete and, especially, serving the state's residents who are the potential customers for insurance meeting the law's criteria.

In accomplishing these and other functions, exchanges must address a number of important issues. These include the following:

- *Adverse selection*—As noted earlier, it is critical that large numbers of healthy people buy insurance through the exchanges and that they be well distributed among competing insurers. Since they can be expected to use relatively few and relatively inexpensive services, enrolling them should provide insurers with enough funds to pay for the care used by less healthy people. Jost reports that adverse selection—that is, when healthy people refrain from buying insurance, leaving the market disproportionately to high users of services—is "the single most important reason" that many exchanges failed in the past.[29] The risk of adverse selection will increase if coverage is easily available to individuals and small groups outside the exchange, and the exchange becomes a high-risk pool as a result.

Fortunately, a number of conditions will reduce the probability that this happens even though they do not completely eliminate the possibility of adverse selection against the exchange. First, individuals are required to have "minimum essential coverage," which will discourage people from avoiding insurance altogether. Second, most reforms apply within and outside the exchange, so there will be less ability for insurers to offer deals outside the exchange that attract large numbers of young, healthy people because the less expensive offerings are less generous. Third, plans for individuals and small groups, whether offered within an exchange or outside it, must cover defined "essential health benefits," and deductibles cannot exceed $2,000 for individuals and $4,000 for families. Fourth, except for enrollees in grandfathered plans, insurers must treat all individual enrollees as a single pool and small-group enrollees as another single pool. Or a state may elect to combine them into one single pool. Fifth, the ACA includes risk-adjustment programs that should reduce adverse selection against the exchange. If plans outside the exchange attract a significantly healthier population than plans within the exchange, the outside group will need to compensate the inside group. And, finally, the subsidies intended to make insurance more affordable will be available only to individuals enrolled in plans through the exchanges.

- *Numbers of participants*—It is important to have large numbers of participants both in absolute terms and as a percentage of insured residents of the state. The reasons are that the potential for new subscribers will attract insurers to offer policies through the exchange, and large numbers will both give the exchange more bargaining power with insurers and increase the probability of having both a diverse risk pool and a stable market.

- *Market coverage and structure*—Should the state have separate risk pools for small groups and individuals? Is the state's potential market large enough to produce enough subscribers that insurers will want to offer policies for sale through the exchange? Alternatively, small states might do better by combining into regional exchanges, and very large states, especially if they have different cost structures for the health care system in different parts of the state, might do well to create substate exchanges.

- *Competition; choice without complexity; transparency and disclosure*—One of the critical underlying ideas of these exchanges is that insurers will compete with one another and will innovate to offer better plans at lower cost than they would otherwise. Assuming that is the case, the challenge for the exchange is to make sure the consumers have accurate information on which to compare plans and that the information is clear enough to facilitate those comparisons on the handful of key dimensions. Too many differences can create "information overload" and be too confusing for consumers to make informed decisions. At the same time, firms must be required to disclose relevant information about their insurance products on which choices can be made and to do so in a format that contributes to rational decisions.

- *Administrative costs*—To perform all these functions and create a strong market will require funds. Yet, at the same time, the exchanges will want to keep costs down—their own and those of the insurers. High administrative costs will reduce the potential savings.

- *Administering subsidies and mandates*—Subsidies will be available under the law for those who need them to be able to afford insurance, and the exchanges will play critical roles in administering them. In addition, it can be expected that some people will move back and forth between coverage offered through the exchange and the state's Medicaid or Children's Health Insurance Program (CHIP). Therefore, another key function will be to work closely with those other programs to ensure seamless coordination for the benefit of affected state residents.

- *Relationships with employers*—In addition to coordination with state agencies, the exchanges must also be aware of their relationships with small employers that might offer coverage through the exchange. Good employer relationships will help to grow an exchange's market and make it more attractive for insurers.

These notes barely scratch the surface of one of the key elements of the Affordable Care Act. The exchanges are central to expansion of good, affordable coverage to employees of small firms and to individuals. Two recent reports from the Commonwealth Fund illustrate not only the variety of issues that arise in creating the exchanges but also the variety of choices faced by the states on all of them.[30] Rosenbaum and her colleagues describe choices made by the legislatures in thirteen states and the District of Columbia in crafting the enabling laws that will guide decision making during the implementation process. Hall and Swartz provide detail about considerations at play in the choices made in three of those states (California, Colorado, and Maryland), as well as the decisions they had yet to make, in actually implementing their health insurance exchanges. Among the many issues to be resolved are the following: the structure of the health insurance exchange entity; membership of the governing bodies; conflict-of-interest provisions; whether to create separate exchanges for individual and small-group markets or a single one; whether the exchange should act as an active purchaser or permit any willing firm to offer coverage; coordination with Medicaid and the Child Health Insurance Program (CHIP); how to protect the exchange against adverse selection; how to ensure the exchange's financial sustainability; and the role of brokers.

For us, the central point is that the choices the exchanges make will be critical in determining the extent to which they succeed in meeting the law's ambitious goals. It is likely that in making them, they—and the legislators who will be crafting state-enabling legislation—will be subject to the influence of lobbyists and other representatives of the various stakeholder groups, including insurers, small businesses, and the variety of provider groups. Moreover, these forces are likely to play out differently in different states, so, in the end, residents of some states may fare better under the law than those in others. As a result, judgments about the law's effects are likely to be more complicated than if we were dealing with a single national program.

ACCOUNTABLE CARE ORGANIZATIONS

Just as the goal to increase access to health care coverage depends primarily on the individual mandate and Medicaid expansion provisions of the ACA, the goal to improve the quality of care and reduce its cost depends largely on accountable care organizations (ACO). They are the subject of this section.

Let's be clear, first, that although the theory supporting the idea behind ACOs is strong, even compelling, there is very little real evidence to date that—when spread throughout the country—they will accomplish the daunting goals with which they are burdened.

The experience of a number of exemplary organizations is encouraging, but leaves unanswered what will happen when the large number of medical practices struggling just to make ends meet try to emulate the trail blazers. Yet improving the quality of care and bringing costs under control throughout the system depends on their succeeding, as well.

The challenges are these: Can ACOs be created throughout the country which provide high-quality care that both is reliable and continues to evolve with scientific developments? And will the aggregation of all these ACOs really increase the probability that medical care will be of high quality, that fewer errors will be made, and that costs will be contained throughout the system?

In this section, first, we will set the stage by reviewing the problems that ACOs are intended to solve. Then we will define accountable care organizations. Third, we will describe how they are expected to accomplish their goals. Finally, we will review the limited literature regarding the experience of organizations that most closely resemble ACOs and look at several current demonstrations. Since these demonstrations are still in progress, however, the emphasis here will be not on results, but on the challenges they face.

Setting the Stage

First, let's recall the health system problems related to quality and spending. Many people get very good medical care from well-trained professionals practicing in well-equipped facilities. But whether or not you are one of the lucky patients who gets that care depends on a variety of mostly nonclinical factors. Most providers operate under severe financial constraints and feel pressure to see more patients and provide more services to each one in order to increase their revenues. At first glance, this appears to be a sensible strategy for provider organizations in part because, since most care is paid for on a fee-for-service basis, they earn separate fees for each service provided. Also, it is easy to implement and requires no changes to current operating practices. But it also is short-sighted because the strategy cannot be sustained over time.

Even with that extra revenue generated by providing more services to more patients, many practice organizations are unable to keep up to date on the latest evidence-based treatments or to replace old, outdated equipment. Further, the tension generated by the financial uncertainty produced by those conditions contributes to avoidable errors, unnecessary services, duplicate services, and other degradations in the standard of care that doctors and other professionals want to deliver.

The financial constraints arise in part because many patients are uninsured or underinsured.

Doctors in small private practices may refuse to treat uninsured patients altogether and encourage them to seek care in hospital emergency departments. And doctors practicing in hospitals where uninsured patients must be treated are often encouraged to limit their time with each patient in order to minimize the financial loss—even in those states which set aside funds for uncompensated care.

In the meantime, private insurers that cover most adult Americans under the age of sixty-five tend to pay higher fees than those paid by public-sector programs, especially Medicaid. They need to find ways to limit their outlays because their profits (or surpluses in the case of not-for-profit firms) are what remains from their premium and investment income after they pay for care and other expenses. One way insurers deal with their own set of pressures is by making it harder for providers of care to be compensated for the services they provide. Thus they require many services to be approved prior to being provided, delay paying even for services that were provided to patients whose coverage was verified beforehand, or in some cases even refuse to pay altogether.

The ACA is designed to reduce these problems by requiring almost everyone to have health insurance and by prohibiting some of the tactics (such as rescission) most harmful to patients that private insurers were using to reduce their outlays on care. If almost everyone has coverage and insurers cannot cancel it when people get sick, the probability increases that providers will really be paid for their work. They may still complain about the rates of payment, but knowing that compensation is coming will reduce the uncertainty about payment and give them the opportunity at least to work on developing better processes for delivering care to their patients.

The care improvement goals include increasing the chances that *appropriate* tests are ordered and provided, that *correct* diagnoses are made, and that *beneficial services* are delivered to patients. Given the explosion of medical knowledge in recent years, doctors and other clinicians need to draw on ever-changing evidence-based information in making choices that increase the chances that the clinical objectives are achieved. The probability of making good choices increases with the use of the latest health information technology (IT)—electronic medical records, electronic ordering of tests and prescriptions, and automated decision support systems. Yet to date IT tools have been diffusing very slowly throughout the country—in large part because while providers bear the cost, others reap the gains. Moreover, the versions of particular IT tools on the market vary in the degree to which they can be helpful.[31]

It is expected that the desired results will be more likely to occur if clinicians—perhaps with payers—organize themselves into accountable care organizations. We turn next to a consideration of ACOs.

What Are Accountable Care Organizations?

Accountable care organizations are legal entities that take responsibility for meeting the medical care needs of their patients and are willing to be held accountable—with financial consequences—for doing so. If they succeed in meeting targeted quality and cost measures for their population of patients, care will cost less and, by sharing in the financial saving with payers, they can earn more. The expectation is that this opportunity to earn more will be enough to stimulate provider organizations to invest in the technology and care processes that can produce quality improvements and contain costs.

ACOs are composed of providers and suppliers of services, the people who deliver the care their patients need. In turn, those providers and suppliers are organized in such a way as to facilitate their ability to deliver high-quality care time after time (that is, reliably). One important goal is to reduce the natural variation in services provided to patients with similar conditions by developing standard processes of care that rely on available research-based knowledge. Modern information systems that contain records of the enrolled patients' health conditions and services received can help a practice's clinicians to develop common clinical processes they all can follow. Since most doctors tend to think they are doing just what their patients need, data generated by those information systems can be analyzed to show skeptical physicians that indeed there is a higher degree of variation than they think in the patterns of services they and their colleagues actually provide to patients with similar conditions. Acknowledging that variation is the first step on the road to reducing it. Then, if the information system also contains a decision support component, which is a store of evidence-based choices for common symptom sets and diagnoses, those same doctors can adopt sensible changes in the services they provide to those patients. The resulting revised care processes then will have been chosen by the providers themselves aided by that information. And since they are based on data about the effectiveness of services, they increase the chances that the clinical goals—of providing effective services to patients efficiently—will be met.

ACOs are designed to overcome conditions endemic to the traditional fee-for-service U.S. health care system, which rewards "volume, growth, and intensity" of services regardless of the value they produce.[32] That system also discourages the introduction of cost-saving innovations (such as electronic medical records) because, as noted, providers bear the costs of adoption, implementation, and maintenance while it is the insurers that reap the benefits of lower costs and reduced duplication of services.

ACOs enroll patients who agree to obtain their care from the ACO's providers. Eventually, the ACO will be paid a fee for each patient enrolled (rather than a fee for each service provided), thus creating an incentive to enroll more patients. Then if the ACO can provide services that cost less than its revenues, it will get to keep the difference. That creates a powerful incentive for the organization's professionals to invest in developing new standard caregiving processes—even though, in the current system, when the clinicians are meeting to review data and make policy choices, they are not earning money for themselves or the organization. During the transition period from today's fee-for-service arrangements to an eventual prepayment model, the ACOs can continue to be paid fee-for-service. In that period, a target expenditure level can be set, and if they can deliver needed services for less than that amount, they can share in the savings with the payer. As already noted, that possibility is intended to provide a strong incentive for the ACO to invest in creating new care processes that permit the practice's clinicians to take good care of their patients for less than the target amount.

ACOs appear in the Affordable Care Act as a "Medicare shared savings program."[33] The law uses federal control of Medicare and the federal budget to promote "accountability for a patient population." It makes funds available to groups willing to sign agreements to act as ACOs. The purposes are to coordinate "items and services under parts A and B [of Medicare]," and to encourage "investment in infrastructure and care processes" leading to "high quality and efficient service delivery."

To qualify for participation in the shared savings program, an ACO must meet a number of requirements, including the following:

- It must be willing to become accountable for the quality, cost, and overall care of the Medicare fee-for-service beneficiaries assigned to it by the Secretary of HHS.

- It must enter an agreement with the Secretary of HHS to participate in the program for at least three years.

- It must have a formal legal structure that allows the organization to receive and distribute payments for shared savings to participating providers of services and suppliers.

- It must have the capacity (as measured by the number of primary care professionals) to care for at least five thousand Medicare beneficiaries assigned to it.

- It must have a leadership and management structure that includes clinical and administrative systems.

- It must define processes to promote evidence-based medicine and patient engagement, report on quality and cost measures, and coordinate care.

- It must be able to submit data required by the Secretary of HHS to evaluate the quality of care furnished by the ACO, including data on transitions across health care settings (that is, when patients move between physicians, hospitals, nursing homes, and other providers).

Besides producing better care for Medicare patients and lower costs for the program, another important objective of the Medicare shared savings program is to learn from the experience and spread those lessons throughout the health care system. Do ACOs actually work as expected? If not, why not? If so, what characteristics differentiate successful ACOs from less successful ones? And how can they be improved? Ultimately the lessons learned from the Medicare experience will spread to care for non-Medicare patients, as well. Indeed, other provisions of the law make funds available for provider organizations to demonstrate new ways of organizing or delivering care to other groups of patients.

Given the widespread preference among both providers and patients for the fee-for-service system they know, the shared savings demonstrations are designed to work with Medicare's traditional fee-for-service payment. Under those arrangements, successful ACOs would share savings that result from meeting financial and quality targets with the Medicare program. It is expected that eventually the program will make the transition to prepaid arrangements.

How Accountable Care Organizations Can Work

One benefit of joining together with other physicians and providers either to form a new ACO or to expand an existing one is to create enough scale so the practice can afford electronic medical records, electronic ordering of tests and prescription drugs, and other beneficial effects of sophisticated information systems, which tend to be expensive and often end up as a net cost to a practice. The latter effect is especially likely to occur in a fee-for-service environment in which the benefits of greater efficiency (fewer duplicate services, for example) tend to accrue to the payers.

A larger practice will need—and probably be able to afford—a professional manager. His (or her) job will include ensuring that the practice has the resources it needs to function effectively and that it negotiates advantageous agreements with payers and organizations that supply goods and services to the now larger practice. Beyond that, and besides acquiring information technology, the manager will want to guide the clinicians through the steps needed to develop standard care processes for providing services to patients with particular common diagnoses. However, to the extent such processes are imposed by managers—as opposed to being self-initiated by the practice's clinicians—they are likely to generate physician resentment of management. The first step therefore will be to use data in the practice's electronic medical record to demonstrate the actual degree of variation in services provided to patients with some common diagnoses, which undoubtedly will be greater than the physicians expect. Then, having done that, the manager will try to guide the organization's physicians to develop evidence-based protocols for treating such patients in the future. After doing this for diabetes, for instance, they can move on to hypertension, low-back pain, or other diagnoses found in large numbers in the practice. Once a protocol is adopted and implemented, the manager will use the data to demonstrate that the result is higher-quality care at lower cost and more net income for the practice. That at least is the hoped-for progression of events.

The fact is, however, that while larger organizations with professional management may have the potential to generate lasting savings as well as improved quality by changing the way care is delivered, producing those hoped-for results is neither easy nor certain. The reason is that once the tools, such as sophisticated information systems, are in place, those results require getting into the substance of clinical diagnosis and treatment decisions. An electronic medical record that simply replaces the paper forms in a metal file cabinet with electronic files and folders will have made the care provided neither more reliable nor less expensive. And most managers, being nonphysicians, are ill-equipped to intervene in clinical decisions in a positive, productive way. To the extent they try, in fact, they may trigger additional resentment from physicians who, rightly, will claim to be the clinical experts in the building. It can be done but it requires considerable care, and it does not come quickly.

As noted, the first challenge is to reduce the often-substantial variation in the diagnosis and treatment patterns of patients with similar conditions. And the first hurdle to overcome usually is to persuade the practice's physicians that, indeed, there *is* considerable variation in practice patterns in the first place. Most physicians believe they are doing what is best for their patients. For a manager to assert that in fact there is considerable variation in the ways that the practice's physicians care for similar patients is likely to be met at first with disbelief. If each doctor is doing what is best for his or her patients, then why are the service patterns leading to accurate diagnoses and effective treatments not similar as well? A manager who insists that variation, not consistency, is the general rule may encounter next statements to the effect of, "If that is true, it must be because my patients are sicker or different in other ways than the other patients even though they have the same diagnoses." Such a claim is hard to overcome, yet the seeds of change are imbedded within the information system if it can be used effectively.

Physicians tend to think of themselves as scientists—not laboratory researchers, perhaps, but professionals whose actions are based on data produced by science. A medical organization with a good information system can reveal exactly what services were provided to each patient with diabetes, for instance. It therefore has the ability to demonstrate the actual amount of variation in practice patterns that results for all the patients in the practice with diabetes or any other diagnosis represented in large numbers of patients. That can be a powerful step if, first, the managers can get the physicians to entertain the possibility of variation and then to accept the validity of the data contained in the practice's own information system. In other words, if they can get the physicians' attention, managers may also be able to get them to acknowledge a greater degree of variation in caring for similar patients than they expected and to consider ways to narrow the differences. (A caveat: the manager needs to begin with diagnoses that are common enough in the practice to be able to generate statistically reliable or stable results. Once that has been done with a handful of diagnoses using data from within the practice, he or she may be able to get the physicians to use data from other sources to develop standard protocols for other diagnoses.)

Having identified the higher-than-expected variation in practice patterns, the effective manager will try to engage the physicians in a process that leads to new patterns based on evidence-based protocols, perhaps ones developed by the practice's physicians themselves. Going through a process of examining the clinical data and results, the physicians may be able to reach agreement on a preferred set of steps to be taken and services to be provided in diagnosing and treating patients with diabetes, for instance, at varying levels of severity. That effort is likely to be time-consuming—and when the practice's physicians are working on it, they are not seeing patients and thus not generating revenues for the practice. One logical conclusion of this situation is that a manager will want to limit the number of physicians participating in the process. Choosing which ones to serve on such a group is another important step. They must be respected enough by their colleagues that the judgments they reach as to steps to be followed in caring for patients with diabetes will be accepted by the others. And then the process will need to be repeated for other common diagnoses.

It is likely that different groups of physicians will be engaged in processes related to different sets of symptoms and diagnoses. If all physicians participate in some of these efforts, not only can the work be spread fairly, but the physicians who went through a sensible process regarding diabetes may be more inclined to accept the conclusions of a different group that has developed a protocol for diagnosing and treating hypertension or low-back pain.

For our purposes, the central question concerns the effects of management's actions on a physician's clinical decisions. The goal is for the practice to reduce its financial burden and ensure its financial viability at the same time that it improves or stabilizes the quality of patient care. The expectation is that it can be achieved to the extent that managers can help the practice to acquire good information technology and then to stimulate the clinicians to engage in the development of treatment protocols based on real data and, by following them, to actually reduce the variation in practice patterns among the group's physicians.

The effects of the ACA regarding quality and costs will be determined first by the extent to which medical practices form or join ACOs and then by the skill with which they attempt to improve the quality of care provided. Obviously, this part of the story has yet to be written. Indeed, it will take years to develop fully.

Early Experience with ACOs and Similar Organizations

We will be able to track the experience of ACOs by following reports from the CMS-sponsored demonstrations and other tests that will develop in the next few years. In fact, Medicare and Medicaid have conducted demonstrations for many years to test the effects of a variety of innovations designed to improve quality and contain costs. Although it antedates passage of the ACA, one such program, the Prepaid Group Practice Demonstrations (PGPD), which operated from 2005 through 2009, had similar goals to those embodied in ACOs. Another ACO pilot program was launched in 2009 by the Brookings Institution and the Dartmouth Institute for Health Policy and Clinical Practice. It involved four provider groups collaborating with private payers to form ACOs. In addition, a number of large private insurers, such as United HealthCare, facing similar cost and quality challenges, are investing in innovation as well. It is too early for these efforts to have produced many results, but some are beginning to appear. What follows is a brief introduction taken from both published sources and personal contacts with leaders in the field.

Many of the projects rely on financial incentives—either shared savings in fee-for-service settings or aligned incentives in prepaid arrangements—and then examination of aggregate results produced by the innovating organizations. They may look at spending per capita or at a variety of quality metrics. The latter usually measure the extent to which patients with a particular diagnosis receive certain specified services or whether the rate at which bad but avoidable things happen is reduced (for example, infections when a central line is put in).

A typical paper appeared recently in JAMA with results from the PGPD.[34] That report found that annual savings per Medicare fee-for-service beneficiary were "modest overall" and that while some of the ten participating institutions achieved substantial savings, others registered no savings at all. The paper leads to two important observations and several questions.

The Observations

1. It is important in a multisite study to examine separately the performance of the individual sites and to not be satisfied with reports of results across all sites.

2. Financial incentives, whatever their influence, are not strong enough by themselves to produce either improved quality of care or reduced spending.

The Questions

1. Why were results better in some places than in others?

2. What actions by health care providers and their patients produced the changes that were recorded?

3. Did those sites in which no changes were found engage in the same activities aimed at improvements as those in which changes were observed?

4. To what extent did the changes that were produced result from either actions taken or processes set in motion by the organization's leaders? As one health care leader put it, Are the physicians engaged in "parallel play" not working together much, or does the organization facilitate productive interactions among them?[35]

5. Assuming the financial incentives got the attention of all the provider groups, or at least their leaders, were they more salient for some groups than for others? If so, why?

6. Did all groups try to respond to the incentives, but some were better at it than others?

7. Were some organization leaders able to produce change, but others, though they tried, not able to do so? If so, why?

8. Were some organizations already doing well by the common quality and cost measures being used? If so, did they have a harder time producing improvements defined as reductions from a prior level of spending or improvements from a baseline state of quality that was considered unsatisfactory care?

These observations and questions also challenge researchers to focus on the *processes* of delivering care as well as the aggregated results. Indeed, it appears that some at least are doing so. The Brookings-Dartmouth group, now including colleagues from UC Berkeley, as well, has plans to focus on internal operations and processes in another project in 2013.[36]

Even before that, however, the researchers make clear that the quality improvement and cost control effort is more complicated than indicated in the few paragraphs earlier that described a process for getting physicians to recognize the variation in utilization patterns and to engage one another in an effort to create a "more standardized" process of care. In another recent paper, the Brookings-Dartmouth group describes the four organizations participating in their project with a focus on the variety of both organization structures and the resulting strategies used to engage the physicians in each. In one, it was critically important that the physician subgroups retain their original identity. So the chosen strategy was to promote "coordination without threatening independent physicians' identity."[37] In another, in which some physicians were organized as a group practice and others were in an IPA, separate strategies were needed for the two subgroups. For some, the focus was on creating an "integrated delivery system" while for others the concept of integration was anathema, so there too the effort was on promoting coordination of care, a lesser type of collaboration. All of the participating organizations were governed in part by prior history, including previous, unsuccessful efforts to improve the delivery of services across multiple providers. Ultimately, although it is too early for any of these groups to have produced outcomes related either to quality of care or costs, it may turn out that some organizational arrangements are more successful on those dimensions than others. Some might even fail altogether. In any event, it will be important to understand why.

All four of the groups in the Brookings-Dartmouth demonstrations are described as having fairly advanced electronic information systems, which presumably can be used to enhance care coordination. Many other physician groups and physician-hospital collaborations will lack that advantage, and so, in addition to the efforts to standardize the processes of care, they may need to adopt, implement, and learn to use electronic medical records and other elements of a mature health care information system. Otherwise, an organization without an electronic medical record and historical care database will need to use other approaches for building consensus to change clinical practices because they will not be able to rely on the ready analysis of prior utilization patterns.

These differences call attention to the fact that the health care organizations that take advantage of funding for demonstration projects tend to be different from other organizations that, on the surface, appear to be similar. Typically, they have leadership that is constantly looking for opportunities to improve their organizations and, in the process, to strengthen their reputations as innovative, forward-looking organizations and leaders.

The combination of forward-looking leadership and advanced capabilities, such as EMR, means that if the ideas have a chance of success, these are the organizations that are most likely to be able to produce it. However, their success in demonstrating the value of the innovations does not mean that those ideas will inevitably spread throughout the entire health care system. Indeed, it is likely to be more difficult for other organizations to produce the same degree of success because they are likely to lack the leadership, the technology, or other characteristics that would ensure fully adopting the innovations, achieving the same degree of accomplishment, and thus having a measurable impact on the entire health care system.

Organizations will start from very different places and have very different histories and capabilities. As a result, we should expect that they will produce—at least at the outset—very different sets of quality-of-care and financial outcomes. And those that succeed in generating the desired outcomes are likely to follow different paths in reaching their goals. A corollary is that evaluations that fail to show dramatic changes in outcomes following a demonstration project of two, three or even four years should not be interpreted to mean that the ideas being tested are without merit. It may just take longer than hoped to produce the desired changes.

Moreover, it should also be pointed out that some types of changes will be easier to achieve than others. For example, a group of orthopedic surgeons performing hip or knee replacements as part of an ACO may be able to both improve quality and lower costs simply by limiting the brands of prostheses they use to a small subset of those that are available on the market. They may need to negotiate among themselves as to which ones should be chosen using the two main criteria of quality and cost, and since all of the surgeons will have their favorites, that might not be easy. But to accomplish that goal requires only a single decision which, if reached, should lead to a clearly measurable endpoint. That type of result should be easier to achieve than members of a medical practice deciding on what multistep protocol to follow in diagnosing and treating patients suspected of having diabetes or reporting low-back pain.[38]

Implicit in the focus on financial rewards for improved performance in the PGPD, as well as in ACOs, is that success is measured not one patient at a time but as aggregated results for the organization as a whole. This may be a difficult concept to grasp for physicians accustomed to practicing in their own offices, perhaps with just one other colleague who shares expenses and call.[39] In deciding how to spend his or her time, that physician is probably thinking about individual patients, one at a time. The organization's leaders, on the other hand, even if they are themselves physicians, are oriented toward the performance of the organization as a whole. Yet that aggregated performance is composed of decisions regarding those same individual patients whom the practitioners see one at a time. Practicing physicians must begin to think not only of the contribution that their patients make to the whole, but also how to redefine their roles and behavior to contribute in a positive way to the organization's outcomes. For example, many patients must be seen by multiple providers who practice in different sites, including hospitals. In the past, the typical primary care physician simply gave the patient a referral to a specialist and let the patient decide whether or not to make an appointment. (Patients might fail to follow through for a variety of reasons, including anxiety about what the specialist will find and want to do as well as the out-of-pocket cost, even for insured patients.) An ACO has a reason to encourage primary care physicians (or members of the physicians' staffs) to follow up with the patient and perhaps to coordinate the patient's ongoing care with the specialist and others. Moreover, his or her redefined roles may include outreach to the patient to facilitate completion of the referral as well as ongoing follow-up. Whether the physician makes phone calls or sets up processes in the practice that lead others—such as nurses—to follow up adds still another dimension. Yet while this is certainly true, the Brookings-Dartmouth researchers found that, in some cases, local physicians do not identify with the "nascent ACO" as a new organization and will not respond positively to an assertion that certain behaviors are necessary because of the ACO's contractual obligations to a payer.[40]

This summary should make clear what a daunting task it will be to produce improved quality and contain costs in many individual care-giving organizations, not to mention in the system as a whole. Nonetheless, proponents can support their confidence in ACOs not just with theory but also with the reported experience of exemplary organizations whose leaders have been able to guide them to new heights of accomplishment.[41] On the basis of this experience, it is reasonable to say, therefore, that organizations with the characteristics of ACOs have been able to achieve strong results in both the quality of care and cost realms. The question is, Are these results attributable primarily to the defining characteristics of ACOs or to the leadership and special characteristics of the organizations in question?

This is an important distinction because the fact is that most health care organizations do not even attempt to do what the Geisingers, Cleveland, or Mayo Clinics and a handful of other such organizations have achieved. Further, over the years, many funded health care projects have demonstrated the value of a promising idea that then did not travel well when the attempt was made to take it beyond the originators. Some organizational leaders are always looking for new opportunities, so that when demonstration funds are made available, they put together teams to create approvable projects. Others tend to "stick to their knitting" and focus primarily on the details of current operations in order to ensure near-term survival.

In their ACO pilot program, which began in 2009, the Brookings-Dartmouth researchers described the characteristics of the organizations, organizational capabilities and structures that influence movement toward accountable care, the stages of the ACO evolution, and common challenges and opportunities. They argue that the organizations' path toward accountable care is influenced by the local social context, provider organizational capabilities, capabilities of the organization's partners and stakeholders, and payer-provider relationships. So, for example, the diverse provider and payer organizations involved in any particular site need to establish a strong degree of trust in order to develop an effective collaboration that can create or strengthen care delivery structures, share clinical and financial data, and establish mutually beneficial formal agreements.

In addition, provider organizations vary dramatically in their capabilities. The Brookings-Dartmouth researchers found that the presence of strong, committed executive leaders and an executive steering committee that can assist in developing the necessary buy-in from the organization's physicians were critical in all four demonstration sites. Absolutely central is the active engagement of individual physicians, since they are most directly responsible for the organization's patient care. The strategies used to engage the physicians included the following: offering financial rewards, highlighting the ACO's fit with professional values, and building on existing trustful relationships. To expand and strengthen the organization's ability to coordinate patient care, some sites leveraged existing information technology, care management, and care improvement infrastructures while others created new programs to coordinate care effectively.

Relationships between physicians, hospitals, payers, and other provider organizations are crucial if the organization is to assume accountability for all of a patient's care. Some have well-established, effective relationships; others do not and will need to build them.

For an organization to assume responsibility for all of its patients' care, patients need first to be attributed to those organizations and even to particular physicians within them. Processes need to be established to accomplish that result, which can lead to patient-provider relationships that both parties can accept and work with.

CONCLUSION

As I have tried to demonstrate, the Patient Protection and Afford-able Care Act addresses all of the major problems facing the U.S. health care system. And although in the best of all possible worlds more direct approaches to the desired changes might have been adopted, the ACA has provisions and tools that can facilitate truly dramatic improvements in the system. That outcome is not a fore-gone conclusion, however, because it depends on so many actions yet to be taken by a host of different actors. Indeed, it is likely that the same statement would be made about any health care reform law that Congress might have passed. We should therefore be grateful to President Obama for his persistence and for the skill of Speaker Nancy Pelosi and Senate Leader Harry Reid in finding the votes to adopt such positive reform legislation—which so many who went before them failed to do. This is even though, as the ACO discussion indicates, systemwide change will be hard to achieve—in part because it is the aggregation of often-difficult changes in thousands of organizations, large and small. Let us hope that those on whom the actual accomplishments of the law will depend will be equally committed to making the law work and have the skill to succeed at that daunting task. If they do, then, as citizens who depend on the health care system, we will all benefit.

NOTES

CHAPTER ONE

1. Jennifer Haberkorn, "Health Policy Brief: Employers and Health Care Reform," *Health Affairs* (March 9, 2011): 1–4.

2. The Kaiser Commission on Medicaid and the Uninsured, *The Uninsured: A Primer: Key Facts About Americans Without Health Insurance* (Washington, D.C., and Menlo Park, CA: The Kaiser Family Foundation, October 2012).

3. Jonathan Cohn, *Sick: The Untold Story of America's Health Care Crisis—and the People Who Pay the Price*. (New York: Harper-Collins, 2007.)

4. Jon R. Gabel, Roland McDevitt, Ryan Lore, Jeremy Pickreign, Heidi Whitmore, and Tina Ding, "Trends in Underinsurance and the Affordability of Employer Coverage, 2004–2007," *Health Affairs Web Exclusive* (June 2, 2009): w595–w606, available at http://content.healthaffairs.org/content/28/4/w595.ful.html, accessed February 7, 2013.

5. Reed Abelson and Milt Freudenheim, "Even the Insured Feel Strain of Health Costs," *New York Times*, May 4, 2008.

6. The information presented here comes from the following sources: Sean P. Keehan, Gigi A. Cuckler, Andrea M. Sisko, Andrew J. Madison, Sheila D. Smith, Joseph M. Lizonitz, John A. Poisal,

and Christian J. Wolfe, "National Health Expenditure Projections: Modest Annual Growth Until Coverage Expands and Economic Growth Accelerates," *Health Affairs* 31, no. 7 (2012): 1600–1612; National Center for Health Statistics, *Health: United States, 2011: With Special Feature on Socioeconomic Status and Health* Hyattsville, MD: NCHS, 2012), Table 129, page 377; The Kaiser Commission on Medicaid and the Uninsured, *The Uninsured*; Cathy Schoen, Michelle M. Doty, Ruth H. Robertson, and Sara R. Collins, "Affordable Care Act Reforms Could Reduce the Number of Underinsured U.S. Adults by 70 Percent," *Health Affairs* 30, no. 9 (2011): 1762–1771.

7. Wendell Potter, "Death Panels: Fact and Fiction," *Huffington Post*, March 21, 2011.

8. National Committee for Quality Assurance, *State of Health Care Quality, 2011* (Washington, D.C.: NCQA, 2011).

9. Michael Shwartz, David W. Young, and Richard Siegrist, "The Ratio of Costs to Charges: How Good a Basis for Estimating Costs?" *Inquiry* 32 (Winter 1995–96): 476–481.

10. The Emergency Medical Treatment and Active Labor Act (EMTALA), which Congress passed in 1986 as part of the Consolidated Omnibus Budget Reconciliation Act (COBRA), requires hospitals to provide care to anyone needing emergency health care treatment regardless of citizenship, legal status, or ability to pay.

11. Stephen M. Davidson and Janelle Heineke, "Toward an Effective Strategy for the Diffusion and Use of Clinical Information Systems," *Journal of the American Medical Informatics Association* 14, no. 3 (May-June 2007): 361–367. See also Melinda Beeuwkes Buntin, Matthew F. Burke, Michael C. Hoaglin, and David Blumenthal, "The Benefits of Health Information Technology: A Review of the Recent Literature Shows Predominantly Positive Results," *Health Affairs* 30, no. 3 (2011): 464–471.

12. Richard J. Baron, Elizabeth L. Fabens, Melissa Schiffman, and Erica Wolf, "Electronic Health Records: Just Around the

Corner? Or Over the Cliff?" *Annals of Internal Medicine* 143 (2005): 222–226.

13. Mark Pauly, "Is Medical Care Different?" in *Competition in the Health Care Sector: Past, Present, and Future*, ed. Warren Greenberg, 11–35 (Germantown, MD: Aspen Systems Corporation, 1978).

14. R. A. Berenson and E. C. Rich, "US Approaches to Physician Payment: The Deconstruction of Primary Care," *Journal of General Internal Medicine* 25, no. 6 (June 2010): 613–618. See also James Robinson, "Theory and Practice in the Design of Physician Payment Incentives," *Milbank Memorial Fund Quarterly* 79, no. 2 (2001): 149–177.

15. Martin Roland, Sowmya R. Rao, Bonnie Sibbald, et al., "Professional Values and Reported Behaviours of Doctors in the USA and UK: Quantitative survey," *BMJ Quality & Safety* (2011), doi: 10.1136/bmjqs.2010.048173, Table 2, available at http://quality safety.bmj.com/site/about/unlocked.xhtml, accessed January 19, 2013.

16. Edmund D. Pellegrino and Arnold S. Relman, "Professional Medical Associations: Ethical and Practical Guidelines," *Journal of the American Medical Association* 282, no. 10 (September 8, 1999): 984–986, quote on page 984.

17. David J. Rothman, "Medical Professionalism—Focusing on the Real Issues," *New England Journal of Medicine* 342, no. 17 (April 27, 2000): 1284–1286, quote on page 1284.

18. Matthew K. Wynia, Stephen R. Latham, Audiey C. Kao, Jessica W. Berg, and Linda L. Emanuel, "Medical Professionalism in Society," *New England Journal of Medicine* 341, no. 21 (November 18, 1999): 1612–1616, quote on page 1612.

19. Pauly, "Is Medical Care Different?"

20. For an expanded discussion of these points, see Stephen M. Davidson, "Open Questions Concerning Influences on Clinical Decision Making," *Journal of Ambulatory Care Management* 36, no. 2 (March 2013): 88–107.

CHAPTER TWO

1. For a list of provisions and their effective dates, see the Commonwealth Fund's website, available at http://www.common wealthfund.org/Health-Reform/~/media/Files/Publications/ Other/2010/CMWF_Overview_Timeline_20102018.pdf, accessed January 19, 2013.

2. James C. Robinson, "The Commercial Health Insurance Industry in an Era of Eroding Employer Coverage," *Health Affairs* 25, no. 6 (2006): 1475–1486.

3. U.S. Government Accountability Office, *Affordable Care Act*, section 6301, available at http://www.gao.gov/about/hcac/ pcor_sec_6301.pdf, accessed February 7, 2013.

4. See the PCORI website at www.pcori.org, accessed January 19, 2013.

5. *Patient-Centered Outcomes Research*, PCORI, www.pcori.org/ reserach-we-support/pcor, accessed February 7, 2013.

6. Ibid.

7. Henry J. Aaron, "The Independent Payment Advisory Board— Congress's 'Good Deed,'" *New England Journal of Medicine* 364, no. 25 (June 23, 2011): 2377–2379.

CHAPTER THREE

1. One could also make the argument that in fact the justice who made that comment was wrong, that the decision to not buy coverage is not rational because everyone's probability of needing services, even expensive ones, is greater than zero. Since that is the case, the unlucky ones who turn out to need care will have lost the chance to buy insurance and instead will face the full cost of the services they use.

2. Jeffrey Toobin, "Comment: To Your Health," *The New Yorker*, July 9, 2012.

3. Paul Starr, *Remedy and Reaction: The Peculiar American Struggle Over Health Care Reform* (New Haven, CT: Yale University Press, 2011), 226.

4. Ibid.

5. David Blumenthal and James A. Morone, *The Heart of Power: Health and Politics in the Oval Office* (Berkeley, CA: University of California Press, 2009.) See also Mark A. Peterson, "It Was a Different Time: Obama and the Unique Opportunity for Health Care Reform," *Journal of Health Politics, Policy and Law* 36, no. 3 (June 2011): 429–436.

6. James A. Morone, "Big Ideas, Broken Institutions, and the Wrath at the Grass Root," *Journal of Health Politics, Policy and Law* 36, no. 3 (June 2011): 375–385.

7. Ibid., 377.

8. Ibid.

9. Ibid.

10. Ibid.

11. Stephen M. Davidson, *Still Broken: Understanding the U.S. Health Care System* (Stanford, CA: Stanford University Press, 2010).

12. Jill Quadagno, *One Nation Uninsured: Why the U.S. Has No National Health Insurance* (New York: Oxford University Press, 2005), at page 12.

13. Ibid., see pages 12–16.

14. Theda Skocpol, *Boomerang: Clinton's Health Security Effort and the Turn Against Government in U.S. Politics* (New York: W.W. Norton, 1996), 146.

15. For more detail about passage of the ACA, readers can consult the following sources: Jonathan Oberlander, "Long Time Coming: Why Health Reform Finally Passed," *Health Affairs* 29, no. 6 (June 2010): 1112–1116; James A. Morone, "Presidents and Health Reform: From Franklin D. Roosevelt to Barack Obama," *Health Affairs* 29, no. 6 (June 2010): 1096–1100; Peterson, "It Was a Different Time: Obama and the Unique Opportunity for Health Care Reform"; Starr, *Remedy and Reaction*; Lawrence R. Jacobs and Theda Skocpol. *Health Care Reform and American Politics: What Everyone Needs to Know* (New York: Oxford University Press, 2010.

16. "Presidents and Health Reform," 1097.

17. Ibid., 1115.

18. Jacob S. Hacker, "Why Reform Happened," *Journal of Health Politics, Policy and Law* 36, no. 3 (June 2011): 437–441, at page 438.

19. Oberlander, "Long Time Coming," 1114.

20. Starr, *Remedy and Reaction*, at 232.

21. Peterson, "It Was a Different Time," 436.

22. Ibid., at page 430.

23. Ibid.

24. Ibid.

25. These included Mary Landrieu of Louisiana, Blanche Lincoln of Arkansas, and Ben Nelson of Nebraska.

CHAPTER FOUR

1. Rogan Kersh, "Health Reform: The Politics of Implementation," *Journal of Health Politics, Policy and Law* 36, no. 3 (June 2011): 613–623, at 614.

2. Ibid., 614.

3. Ibid., 614.

4. Ibid., 614.

5. Benjamin D. Sommers and Arnold M. Epstein, "Why States Are So Miffed About Medicaid—Economics, Politics, and the "Woodwork Effect," *New England Journal of Medicine* 365, no. 2 (July 14, 2011): 100–102.

6. Benjamin D. Sommers and Arnold M. Epstein, "Medicaid Expansion—The Soft Underbelly of Health Care Reform?" *New England Journal of Medicine* 363, no. 22 (November 25, 2010): 2085–2087.

7. Kaiser Commission on Medicaid and the Uninsured, *Performance Measurement Under Health Reform: Proposed Measures for Eligibility and Enrollment Systems and Key Issues and Trade-Offs to Consider* (Washington, D.C.: Kaiser Family Foundation, December 2011), 3.

8. Ibid.

9. Ibid.

10. Abby Goodnough, "Insurance Rebates Seen as Selling Point for Health Law," *New York Times*, July 30, 2012.

11. Health Care for America Now, *New Federal Health Law's Insurance Premium Rules Will Control Costs for Families, Businesses*, Washington, D.C., July 22, 2010, available at http://healthcarefor americanow.org/2010/07/22/hcan-report-new-federal-health -law's-insurance-premium-rules-will-control-costs-for-families -businesses, accessed January 19, 2013.

12. "Credible" insurers are those that are large enough to be subject to the medical loss ratio requirement.

13. Kaiser Family Foundation, *Explaining Health Care Reform: Medical Loss Ratio (MLR)*, publication #8282, February 2012, available at www.kff.org/healthreform/8282.cfm, accessed January 19, 2013.

14. Timothy Stoltzfus Jost, "Reflections on the National Association of Insurance Commissioners and the Implementation of the Patient Protection and Affordable Care Act," *University of Pennsylvania Law Review* 159, no. 6 (June 2011): 2043–2060.

15. Ibid., 2047.

16. Ibid., 2050.

17. Ibid., 2053.

18. Ibid.

19. Ibid., 2051.

20. Ibid., 2052.

21. Eugene Bardach and Robert A. Kagan, *Going By the Book: The Politics of Regulatory Unreasonableness* (with a new Introduction) (New Brunswick, NJ: Transaction Publishers, 2002), 44–45. (Originally published in 1982 by Temple University Press.)

22. John D. Rockefeller IV, Letter to Commissioner Jane L. Cline, July 20, 2010.

23. Ibid., 3.

24. Ibid., 4.

25. Ibid.

26. Ibid.

27. This section draws primarily on the following sources: Jon Kingsdale and John Bertko, "Insurance Exchanges Under Health Reform: Six Design Issues for the States, *Health Affairs* 29, no. 6 (2010): 1158–1163; and Timothy Stoltzfus Jost, *Health Insurance Exchanges and the Affordable Care Act: Key Policy Issues*, The Commonwealth Fund, July 15, 2010, available at http://www.common wealthfund.org/Publications/Fund-Reports/2010/Jul/Health -Insurance-Exchanges-and-the-Affordable-Care-Act.aspx, accessed January 19, 2013.

28. As noted in Chapter Seven of Stephen M. Davidson, *Still Broken: Understanding the U.S. Health Care System* (Stanford, CA: Stanford University Press, 2010), competition is unlikely to produce the hoped-for benefits.

29. Jost, *Health Insurance Exchange*, 3.

30. Mark A. Hall and Katherine Swartz. *Issue Brief: Establishing Health Insurance Exchanges: Three States' Progress* (New York: The Commonwealth Fund, July 2012), publication #1611; Sara Rosenbaum, Nancy Lopez, Taylor Burke, and Mark Dorley, *Issue Brief: State Health Insurance Exchange Laws: The First Generation* (New York: The Commonwealth Fund, July 25, 2012), publication #1616, available at http://www.commonwealthfund.org/Publications/ Issue-Briefs/2012/Jul/State-Health-Insurance-Exchange-Laws.aspx, accessed February 7, 2013.

31. Stephen M. Davidson and Janelle N. Heineke, "Toward an Effective Strategy for the Diffusion and Use of Clinical Information Systems," *Journal of the American Medical Informatics Association* 14 (2007): 361–367.

32. Elliott S. Fisher, Mark B. McClellan, John Bertko, Steven M. Lieberman, Julie J. Lee, Julie L. Lewis, and Jonathan S. Skinner, "Fostering Accountable Health Care: Moving Forward in Medicare," *Health Affairs* 28, no. 2 (2009): w219–w231, published online on January 27, 2009 at http://content.healthaffairs.org/ content/28/2/w219.full.pdf+html.

33. See Section 3022 of the ACA, which was incorporated into the Social Security Act as Section 1899 of Title XVIII, the Medicare title.

34. Carrie H. Colla, David E. Wennberg, Ellen Meara, Jonathan S. Skinner, Daniel Gottlieb, Valerie A. Lewis, Christopher M. Snyder, and Elliott S. Fisher, "Spending Differences Associated with the Medicare Physician Group Practice Demonstration," *Journal of the American Medical Association* 308, no. 10 (September 12, 2012): 1015–1023.

35. Personal communication with Lewis G. Sandy, M.D., Senior Vice President for Clinical Advancement at UnitedHealth Group, September 18, 2012.

36. Personal communications with Elliott Fisher and Stephen Shortell, September 2012.

37. Sara A. Kreindler, Bridget K. Larson, Frances M. Wu, et al., "Implications of Integration in Early Accountable Care Organizations," *The Milbank Quarterly* 90, no. 3 (2012): 457–483, at page 478.

38. Atul Gawande, "Annals of Health Care: Big Med," *The New Yorker*, August 13, 2012, pp. 52–63.

39. Personal communication with Lewis G. Sandy, M.D., Senior Vice President for Clinical Advancement at UnitedHealth Group, September 18, 2012.

40. Kreindler, et al., "Implications of Integration in Early Accountable Care Organizations," at page 457.

41. Examples include the Geisinger Health System, Group Health of Puget Sound, the Mayo Clinic, and the Cleveland Clinic, among others.

Made in the USA
San Bernardino, CA
11 November 2013

DEC 03 2013
12.99